THE
UNTOLD STORY
OF
MI Home products Inc
·····
Inside

MR GEORGE BROWN SR

ISBN: 1-4922-9847-6

ISBN 13: 978-1-4922-9847-2

Inside Corruption of Management in Manufacturing

I started working at MI Metal Products Inc. (which later changed its name to MI Home Product Inc.) in Millen, Georgia, on April 26, 1993. I worked as a glasscutter machine operator. This plant was under the leadership of Mr. Ed Kennel, who was the general manager, and Mr. Lester Wallace, the plant manager. I worked under the supervision of Mr. James Jackson, better known as Roundhead.

Mr. Kennel operated according to the rules and regulations of the company policies and did not follow his own desires, nor did he allow anyone else to influence him into doing something that was wrong or harmful to the company. I worked as a laborer for about two years, and during my two years as a laborer, I encountered a lot of wrong doings by supervisors. Mr. Kennel had departed from the company in Millen, Georgia, at this time.

The company appointed Mr. Terre Snare as the general manager, and Mr. Wallace still held his position as plant manager. In 1995, the company brought in Mr. Strayer to help reshape the company's production. I was promoted to the patio glass house as a supervisor. My job was to straighten out the production and quality of patio glass house and reduce the overtime that had gotten out of control.

Before I was appointed supervisor, the patio door department was in deep overtime. They were working thirty hours a pay period per employee. After I assumed the responsibility, I immediately found that it was unorganized. Mrs. Susie Ann Edwards was the lead person at the time. I tried to keep everybody in the same position that they were in when I took charge. I found myself making some rearrangements after I watched them for a week. I went to Mrs. Edwards and asked her where they were with the work orders, and she told me that she did not know. I therefore asked Ms. LaShawnya Robinson, and she knew, so I placed her as a lead person. I asked Mr. Strayer if I could reorganize the department, and he said that the department was mine. I was to do whatever I needed to do. I immediately took the employees in the glass department and began reorganizing the department for a better flow of production. I placed everyone in the position that I needed him or her to be in for the benefit of the company. My goal was to be able to produce the products on time to the customers.

After that, I went over to the patio door department where it was running up to thirty-plus overtime hours per pay period. In just a month's time, they went down to eight to zero overtime hours. Mr. Doug Biessel was ordering the glass for the patio glass department. He noticed how well organized the department was. He allowed me to order my own glass and materials for the production operation. The production and the quality of the patio glass panels soon caught the eyes of all the plant personnel. The customers also noticed.

Dave Carter and Associates suggested that if MI Home Product Inc. could produce all the doors and parts they needed to provide to their customers, then they would only order their door products from them. The personnel at the plant talked about the cleanliness of the patio glass department. They boasted about how the quality and production had improved by a 100 percent, according to Mr. Hetrick, Mr. Snare, Mr. Strayer, Mr. Ogden, and Mr. Young. Sales were up, and it came to a point where they had to hire a second shift to produce the doors that were ordered by the customers.

They also wanted to hire a second shift for the patio glass house as well. I told them that if they would hire the extra employees that I needed, then they would not need to start a second shift in the patio glass house. It would save the company expenses from hiring the second shift. The patio glass house produced enough panels to keep the first and second shift patio door department in full operation, which could have resulted into hiring a completely full new shift. The patio glass house was producing over a thousand panels per day and had only ten to zero hours of overtime per pay period, compared to five hundred panels per day and the patio door department being in deep overtime with back orders to the customers under the leadership of Mr. Brain Richardson. After the high volume of orders leveled off, they no longer needed the second shift, which resulted into patio glass house having to help pull 450 and 255 glass houses out of deep overtime. This eased the tension off the supervisors in the windows section.

Once all this had taken place, Mr. Strayer stayed only a few more months. They then brought in Mr. Steve Brush as the general manager. He immediately saw the success that the company was having as a result of me being part of the team. Mr. Steve Brush changed the pay scale for all supervisors. They then decided to send me to management seminar classes in Millersburg Pennsylvania, by plane. We stayed in Harrisburg, Pennsylvania, at the Sheraton Inn in 1998 and 1999. I completed both seminars successfully. The reason for the seminar was set off by my performance as a leader in helping landing the Dave Carter and Associates full purchaser account and the number one vendor of the year award from Carolina Builders.

Mr.Hetrich and Mr. Brush saw that I was very beneficial to the company, and they invested in me as any good manager would. I continued to perform and operate throughout the plant to the point that Mr. Brush wanted me to continue helping my fellow window glass house supervisors. I furthered my abilities to perform by attending those seminars.

In the year of 1998 and 1999, we were in the process of purchasing the True Seal Swiggle machine that would produce a finished product when it came out of the machine. This started in the 255/165 series glass house. Mr. Reed allowed me to reward my patio glass house department by giving them a dinner at the expense of the company, for a job well done. We were heading into the right direction of becoming the number one MI plant.

Mr. Brush told me to go over to the 255/165 glass house and see if I could spread some of my blessings over there. At this time, they were in the process of beginning to run production on the newly set up True Seal Swiggle glass house. Mr. Alphonzo Sapp was the acting supervisor, and Mr. Todd Reed and Mr. Peter Atkinson were the production managers. Mr. Peter Atkinson was in charge of getting the right people in position in order to run that department. According to him, he told Mr. Brush that he felt that Mr. Brown would be more qualified to run that department than Mr. Sapp.

During the Thanksgiving weekend, Mr. Todd Reed called me at my home and told me that I needed to come to the plant immediately. I said that I would be there shortly. After I arrived, he told me that as of the following week, I would be the supervisor over the 255/165 glass house. I asked him what happened to Mr. Sapp. He told me that Mr. Sapp had been fired. I asked him for the reason of Mr. Sapp's termination. Mr. Todd Reed told me that he left without permission. I said to myself, "Is that all?" I told Mr. Reed that since Mr. Sapp had not had a violation of any conduct, he at least deserved a suspension. Mr. Reed said it all depended on what Mr. Brush had to say. He said that if it were totally up to him he would be gone. For me, taking the job was not an option, it was a demand.

I never went to school for the training of the True Seal operation as Mr. Sapp did. I took that department and began running it the way Mr. Reed wanted me to run it. The 255 window series and 165 window series at the same time which was for two different departments, and doing it that way was hindering production. Everyone in the department was new to that way of operation and had to learn the way of performing production. When Mr. Atkinson came in, I told him that I needed to run the production my way in order to get anything done, and he asked me what I was talking about. I told Mr. Atkinson that Mr. Reed wanted me to run two different series of glass at the same time, and the employees do not understand the operation. Running the operation that way was only causing confusion, and the glass was getting mixed up. He then told me to run it my way.

The next day I went in and called the employees together for a meeting. I told them that we were no longer going to run two series at one time. We all were in the learning process, and I realized that there were going to be some mistakes, but we would correct and learn from them as we went along. I told them, "There's money to be made, and if you want to take home a decent salary, then we all had to work together to make that happen." I told them that anyone who did not want to be a part of the team should let me know, and I would try to find them a home in another department. I was not worried about production right then. My main concern was for the employees learning all aspects of their jobs. I knew that after that, production would follow. Some of the employees became frustrated. I encouraged them by saying that they were doing a good job and to keep it up. After the week in training, through my encouragement and motivating them, they gained confidence in themselves. Soon production began to pour in.

Mr. Jimmy was my lead person, and I told Mr. Williams it was his job to make sure they had everything that they needed in order to perform their job. He said, "Okay, just tell me what I need to do." As time progressed, I began to look for ways to improve production. I began timing them and continued to encourage them. I held weekly meetings in order to let them know where we were and where we needed to be. The employees told me that they never had a supervisor like me before. They said that Mr. Alphonzo Sapp never had any meetings with them. I told them that these meetings were to let everyone understand where we stand with production and what we needed in order to complete the task that had been set before us.

Every time we had our supervisor morning meeting, it included the regional manager, general manager, and the production manager Mr. Gary Hetrick, who had always complimented me on a job well done. He said the intercepts insulation glass machines supposed to be the fastest producer of units per man-hour, but "George has surpassed it." I was planning on making MI Home Product Inc. the number one unit per man-hour producer in the *True Seal* magazine. I kept on searching for more ways to produce more panels with greater quality. Then it came to me. I called a meeting with the 255/165 glass house. I told them that I had been watching the Swiggle operators. You can Swiggle two units per minute, but due to having to change your guns and your Swiggle, it reduced your production. I told them that I would have Mr. Brush order some backup guns, and Jimmy would keep a gun ready for them at all times and change their Swiggle out. I promised them that they would take home a better salary.

The morale of the employees was more unifying than ever. Then I went to Mr. Brush and told him how we would accomplish more production with a set of backup guns. I explained to him how we could accomplish more production. He agreed and went ahead and ordered the extra guns for me. After I received those extra guns for the line, production shot up. Mr. Hetrick called the *True Seal* magazine and told them that we had surpassed their number one unit per man-hour producer on their front cover. Shortly after my idea to become the number one True Seal producer, the team and I made it become reality. Yes, now it reads that MI Home Product Inc. is the number one unit per man-hour producer in the *True Seal* magazine. I was so proud of my team for helping to achieve such an honor, I decided to give them a dinner in order to show my gratitude for their motivation to break the record of the world.

One day Mr. Todd Reed came to me and asked me if I had to be transferred, would I be willing to transfer? I told him no because I had too much invested in Twin City Georgia at the time. As time passed, Mr. Reed would go out of his way to try to find some fault in me or with my work. I didn't understand why, because my department was the best production department throughout the whole plant. It was the cleanest and the most organized. I ran production on schedule or ahead of schedule, all of my paperwork was turned in on a timely manner, and the supplies that I ordered for my department were always on time.

Mr. Steve Brush, the general manager, asked me to be in charge of ordering all of the other Swiggle glass house's supplies and I said sure, that wouldn't be a problem. He told me to keep up the good work. I said okay, but Mr. Reed kept looking for something to blame me for. He would get down on his knees looking under the machines. I continued trying to figure out why, and then it came to me. He was mad because I had turned down his offer of being relocated to another plant.

Mr. Brush and Mr. Reed came up with a plan to base the supervisor's bonus on. It was called weekly department evaluations housekeeping sheet. The items listed on it were excellent (six points), good (five points), fair (four points), poor (three points), and unacceptable (zero points). I always scored excellent or good. I wasn't troubled by their new system of receiving bonuses. My performance was great, and I knew that I would stay on top of things. Supervisors were known for trying to blame others for their failures, and Mr. Reed was good at it.

I remember one day when Mr. Reed came to me and asked me, "Why are you writing units that you haven't run?" I asked him, "Who told you that lie?" He wouldn't say who told him that. He asked me, "Where is my order for the units out there on the floor?" I told him to hold on for a minute. I went to my desk to get the order. Mr. Reed and I went over the units that were listed on the order, and all the units were there except for two out of fifteen hundred units. I told him that others could have gotten those two units without my knowledge. I always tell my employees to replace anything that gets broken going through the oven. I know that they replace it, because I spot check behind them to make sure that they are following through.

I asked him if Ms. Georgia Golden had carts of broken glass, then tell me where her repair tickets are. I told him that I hadn't received any repair tickets from her. Mr. Reed looked through the repairs that I had, and only saw repairs for the 165 series, which was run by Mr. Rick Lineberry. When all of that failed, they came up with a date stamp plate to put the date on the glass. The maintenance men installed the machine, but the date pad was not ready. It had to be glued to the plate and set for twenty four hours in order to hold in place. Mr. Atkinson told me that Mr. Reed did not like me for some reason. I told him that it's because I would not relocate to another plant at this time, and then Mr. Atkinson told me that I had better watch my back.

The next day Mr. Junior Dailey put the pad on the stamper. I suggested for them to put the machine in the back because it would be one hundred percent actual back there, and she will be able to stamp every panel that comes out complete. I let them know that if they left it up front, we would have some missing due to glass getting broke. Mr. Dailey and Mr. Atkinson told me that it was a great idea, but they would have to get permission from Mr. Reed first because he told them to put it in the front. They went to Mr. Reed and told him about the idea. Mr. Reed asked them whose idea it was. Mr. Dailey and Mr. Atkinson said, "George," and he told them to leave it where it was.

When they came back, they said Mr. Reed said leave it where it was. In a few hours, the pad blew off the glue that they applied. It would not hold the pad on. Mr. Reed put it on hold until they could get in some more glue for the stamp plate. When it came in, they applied glue to it and let it sit overnight. They then put it on the stamp pad, and this time it lasted for about six hours and blew off again. I called the maintenance people back out there to replace it, and it had to sit overnight in order to seal the pad to the stamp plate. After they got the new glue in, it still would not hold the pad on. Mr. Reed became frustrated and tried to blame me for not stamping the glass. I told him that the pad would not stay on there, and it takes twenty-four hours after you glue it before you can use it. Yet he continued to blame me for the pad not holding. I asked him why he was blaming me. I did not order the glue or put it on, the maintenance man did.

At this time we had two other Swiggle glass houses that were running the same type of units that I was running. He did not have a problem with them, even though the glue was not holding the pad down for them either. I told Mr. Atkinson that Mr. Reed was giving me a hard time about something beyond my control and not the other two Swiggle glass houses. He said, "I told you. He's holding something against you for some reason. Just watch yourself." I told him okay.

Mr. Atkinson then told me when he first went to Mr. Brush and Mr. Reed and told them that I was the man for this job, he could not see any way for Mr. Sapp to handle this department. They told him that I could not handle it. Now I had made them out to be liars, and they didn't like it. I told Mr. Atkinson about all the time and dedication I put in trying to help make MI Home Product Inc. become the number one producer of all the MI plants. He said, "They don't care about that either if you got something to do with it. I'm telling you, just continue to watch yourself." I told him okay and thanks.

During this time, Mr. Steve Brush made Mr. Todd Reed his assistant plant manager. Here are some of the copies of facts in order to support my account of my performance during this time as supervisor under the leadership of Mr. Steve Brush and Mr. Todd Reed of MI Home Product Inc.

DEPARTMENT : _George - Black_

COMMENTS

MONTH _Dec. 99_

	excellent-6	good-5	fair-4	poor - 3	unexcept-0
OORS SWEPT					
RGANIZATION					
W MATERIALS					
IISHED GOODS	✓				
UIPMENT					
DATE :						TOTAL __27__

Comments: _Naughlin done in pencil_
Clean under switch over - take off end.

	excellent-6	good-5	fair-4	poor - 3	unexcept-0
OORS SWEPT		✓			
RGANIZATION		✓			
W MATERIALS		✓			
IISHED GOODS		✓			
UIPMENT					
DATE :						TOTAL __27__

	excellent-6	good-5	fair-4	poor - 3	unexcept-0
OORS SWEPT		✓			
RGANIZATION	✓				
W MATERIALS	✓				
IISHED GOODS		✓			
UIPMENT					
DATE :						TOTAL __27__

	excellent-6	good-5	fair-4	poor - 3	unexcept-0
OORS SWEPT					
RGANIZATION					
W MATERIALS					
IISHED GOODS					
UIPMENT					
DATE :						TOTAL ____

	excellent 6	good-5	fair-4	poor - 3	unexcept-0
OORS SWEPT					
RGANIZATION					
W MATERIALS					
IISHED GOODS					
UIPMENT					
DATE :						TOTAL ____

	excellent-6	good-5	fair-4	poor - 3	unexcept-0
OORS SWEPT					
RGANIZATION					
W MATERIALS					
IISHED GOODS					
UIPMENT					
DATE :						TOTAL ____

MONTHLY TOTAL: ____

This has always been my performance, and anything less than this is a false document. The next document is my incentive for March 2000, which will show that my performance has never been an issue to the company before. Everything I did was in the best interests of the company in order to better the production and quality.

MONTHLY INCENTIVE PAY--MILLEN

MONTH: Mar-00

NAME : George Brown
DEPARTMENT : Glass #4 255/165

	BONUS RATE	WEEK 1	WEEK 2	WEEK 3	WEEK 4	WEEK 5	TOTAL MONTH	GOAL	BONUS
UNITS/MAN HOUR	$150	15.24	14.46	16.09	15.52	13.43	14.95	14.00	$150.00
Glass SCRAP	$150	11.1	12	12.2	11.7	13	12.0%	12.5%	$150.00
COST per Glass Pnl	$120	0.99	1	0.92	0.98	0.91	$0.96	$1.00	$120.00
SHIP COMPLETE	$100	99.5%	100.0%	99.5%	99.4%	98.8%	99.4%	98.5%	$100.00
HOUSEKEEPING	$100	28	29	28	29	29	143	104/165	$100.00
OSHA REPORTABLE	$100	0	0	0	0		0	0	$100.00
TOTAL	$720								$720.00

4 week month — 105 to 120 pts. = full bonus   5 week month – 132 to 150 pts. = full bonus
89 to 104 pts. = 1/2 bonus   113 to 131 pts. = 1/2 bonus

My performance is something that I take pride in. Also my employees don't need me to be there for them to turn down a unit that doesn't meet my expectation of quality, because I taught them what I will accept and what I will reject. They sometimes went to other glass house departments to help them out in order for that line to achieve their production. They told the employees on that line, "You mean to tell me that your supervisor lets you send out stuff like this?" They told them yes. My employees told them, "You can't send stuff out like that on George Brown's line. He isn't going to allow us to let grids go off his line looking like that." It had gotten to a point where I had to help other glass houses run production every week or send them some help in order for them to meet their production in a timely manner. I never had a back order due to my performance as a production supervisor, nor did I ever have a complaint from any of MI Home Product customers concerning glass issues. Mr. Hetrick, Mr. Snare, and Mr. Atkinson always had good things to say about my performance.

I remember the time when we had a meeting with the company attorney. Mr. Hetrick told the attorney, "George Brown runs the 255/165 Swiggle glass house. The intercept is supposed to be the number one producer, and George runs circles around it," and everybody just laugh. The meeting consisted of the company polices of safety, sexual harassment, and wrongful termination, telling us that we have to be careful how we fire someone today because people are looking for a reason to sue. That's why it is very important to follow the company's procedures with the proper paperwork. That seminar went in one ear and out the other. I must say that Mr. Gary Hetrick is a good man and believes in following the company polices, but what he doesn't know he just doesn't know. Most of the time the underhanded dealing was done while he was away visiting other plants of the company or it was something that wasn't brought to his attention truthfully. Instead there were deception and lies by the others, such as the plant manager or his assistant. Human resources does not have an excuse, because the original paperwork had to go through him, which is Mr. Lee Wilson. It was his job to make sure that any incident that comes to him is investigated and actual before he takes action, not to take action and then say, "I made a mistake," because most business people are not going to own up to their mistakes.

A lot of the problems that happened at MI Home Products Inc. are because of Mr. Wilson not having enough courage to let the corrupt leadership know that he could not do some of the things that they wanted done in the plant in Millen, Georgia. Due to Mr. Wilson's lack of concern for the benefit of the company, he allowed corruption to go on throughout the plant. He allowed them to layoff good and hard-working people who knew their jobs and were always dependable just to please his friends. He allowed them to put people in positions that he knew they were not qualified for and gave them a high-paying salary. The only thing they did was cost the company money by messing up so much of the materials and having to throw it away due to being cut wrong, which resulted into hundreds of thousands of dollars.

Mr. Wilson allowed them to pay Mr. Steve Landsman's stepson, Mr. Chad Oglesby, a supervisor's salary for being over one janitor. The only thing he did was keep the plant clean, just because he was a friend's stepson. How about his responsibility to the company? They knew the topic and the meaning, which

Mr. Brush said in every morning meeting,but they refused to follow it, which is teamwork meaning all leaders work together.

We were in full production. Due to another one of MI Company's failures, we had to pitch in and help them maintain the Lowe's orders to keep from losing the customer, which put us in overtime. We were over our normal production, which ended up into opening two shifts for the 255/165 Swiggle glass house and the 165 series window line. We had a meeting, and Mr. Steve Brush, Mr. Todd Reed, and Mr. Peter Atkinson told me that we needed to start a new shift and I was going to be over both shifts, the first and the second. He told me to find somebody to run the second shift and go ahead and get the people in that I needed in order to get the job done. I said okay, what would I be responsible for? Mr. Reed said, "Making sure that the second shift has everything that they need in order to make production." He told me that until I got all the people that I needed, I would be making all of his parts for the second shift production and to make preparation for the second shift set up.

I had a meeting with my employees and told them what was in process and what we needed to do in order to make it work. I chose my lead person as Mr. Jimmy Williams for the leadership on the second shift. I told Mr. Williams that I was going to get some people in and start training them how to Swiggle and top, because that's the most important part, and everything went according to plan. Then I start getting the people in and started training them because I only had three weeks to act upon it before the second shift would begin production. They were working against me because of the lack of time to get everybody in and get things set up, but the more they tried to set me up, the more I was determined to succeed. I went ahead and got the people to run and cut glass and boosted up the assembling table in order to meet both the day shift and the night shift production.

When I took payroll my paperwork, Melissa and Belinda said, "George, I do not believe you picked Jimmy for your supervisor at night." I asked them why they said that. They replied, "He is a big liar." I asked them what he lied about. They said, "What is it that he has not lied about?" I told them it would be all right because everything he does had to go through me first. He was all I had at the time. They said, "I hate to tell you but you are going to regret it."

We went ahead and gave Mr. Williams a status change after I got everybody in and got them trained by Mr. David J. Robinson and Mrs. Fayanel Bell. I had a meeting with them and told them what was required of them. I introduced them to Mr. Jimmy Williams as the person in charge of the night shift and said that if there were a problem and Mr. Williams could not handle it, they should feel free to talk to me and I would take care of it. They said okay. I told them that I wasn't worried about production right then, but what I was mostly concerned about was them knowing their job. I was confident that once they learned it, production would come. I also told them that they must realize that we needed good and dependable people. I asked them if there was a problem with anyone getting to work, and they said no. I wanted to make sure that they understood what our goal was and to show them that we could do it. Everyone agreed.

I asked Mr. Jimmy Williams if he have anything to say, and Mr. Williams told them that he was glad to have a good team. He went over their breaks with them, and he said, "Thank you, I'll see you tomorrow night." When we started the night shift, I was given complete control over both shifts and everything ran smoothly. All the orders was completed before time, even the add-on orders, and there were tons of those add-on orders. Everyone followed my instructions and knew what to do. Whether I was there or not, they knew what they could or could not do because I was the one giving them their orders and materials to run in June 2000.

We made our first six million dollars at MI Home Product. At that point, we were on our way to becoming the number one MI plant producer of all MI plants. Mr. Todd Reed then called me in his office and told me that I could not tell Mr. Jimmy Williams how to run his department. I told him that Mr. Williams couldn't run that department on his own, even though he had two grid girls working at night assembling grids. Mr. Reed said that it would be his problem, not mine, so I said okay.

After two weeks Mr. Williams started running the production out of order, and I told Mr. Peter Atkinson and Mr. Todd Reed that Mr. Williams had gotten out of control. He started lying about what he had done, running orders with the wrong grids; he assembled over one hundred and fifty 28x45 9lites that had to be thrown away because they were not assembled right. Mr. Reed said to make them over. The grids that were cut and punched wrong had to be thrown away. The oven was not set right, causing panels to be too thick. We had to punch holes in them and run them through the oven again. He had started falsifying his piece rate sheet, and I had to correct them, which was witnessed by Mr. Peter Atkinson.

When Mr. Williams came in, Mr. Atkinson and I Mr. Brown talked to him about the piece rate sheet. He agreed that he added some glass to it because of the problems they had, and I told him if he had problems, he should not add unfinished units. You can add maintenance pay or send them home if you cannot get the production back up and going. Mr. Atkinson said, "Jimmy, you are going to get yourself in lots of trouble." He told him it would not happen anymore, but I felt that Mr. Reed was behind his action, trying to blame me for the mistakes, because he always wanted to blame me for something that Mr. Williams had done on the night shift. I told him that he told me that I couldn't tell Mr. Williams what to do. I didn't feel that I should be held liable for what Mr. Williams did. He told me that I had been supervisor for a long time, and I needed to know better. I said, "Todd, if I can't be over Mr. Williams and tell him what I want him to do and have everything in my control, how can I be held responsible for something that I have no control over?" He had told me that Mr. Williams would be held responsible for what he does, not me. Mr. Atkinson then told me he would get back with me later and for me to go back to work.

Later on that day, Mr. Steve Brush came down to my department complaining about glass not being counted right. I told him everything that I produce is actual and accounted for, and he asked why was Georgia Golden one hundred and fifty panels short. I told Mr. Brush we ran over two thousand units, 2,850 panels. Of the 2,850 panels that week, I didn't have one repair ticket on any. If you continue to break panels and don't turn them in for repair, at the end you will come up short.

Then we went over to Georgia's department and asked her about the repairs. She said she turned them in, and I asked her then where was her copy? She had not turned it in; she couldn't give us one because there wasn't one. Mr. Brush jumped off the panels being short and two blocks not being put in the glass in order to keep the panels from breaking, and I told him the glass that I ran had blocks in them. The glass that did not have blocks was what Mr. Williams ran the prior night. He didn't even say a word. Not only didn't Mr. Williams put any blocks in his finished good glass, but neither did Mr. Joseph Scroggins or Mr. Alphonzo Sapp, and they also operated the Swiggle glass houses. Mr. Brush said, "I bet the next time I come back here, you better have blocks in the glass or you're fired." I asked Mr. Atkinson how could Mr. Brush and Mr. Reed blame me for something I had no control over. They had told me that the night shift wasn't any of my concern, but every time I turned around they were trying to blame me for something the night shift did. Mr. Atkinson said, "George, I told you that Mr. Brush and Mr. Reed didn't like you because you made them out to be liars."

I tried everything I knew to fire Ms. LaShawnya Robinson due to her misconduct on the job, and Mr. Todd Reed told me to work with her because she was young. Then he ask if she was a good worker. I told him yes, but she causes to much trouble. He said, "George, just work with her," and I told him okay. I ended up having to write her up several times. I gave her a suspension, thinking that it might put her on the right track, but even that didn't do any good. Mr. Gary Ogden terminated her after she had gotten mad and walked out of the plant. He turned around and put her back on my line. I didn't know whether they were trying to help me or hurt me; I do know whatever they were doing, it wasn't good for the line.

Later on I transferred her to a specialty glass house department. The next thing I knew she was back in my department, and I was told to do a department status change. I went to payroll and did the change, and then I went to the human resource office and asked him why they put her back on my line. Mr. Atkinson said that was what Todd wanted. Then later on I had her transferred to Mr. Williams's department on the night shift. Mr. Williams ran orders so out of order that it caused my department to work on a Saturday. There wasn't anything said, and he wasn't written up for messing up glass that had to be thrown away. The very next week Mr. Williams did the same thing, except this time it was the next morning load date and he had the glass all mixed up. Half of it did not run. There was scrap glass everywhere, and half of what he did run wasn't any good due to the fact that the grid bars were too far off from the Swiggle sealant.

I called Mr. Reed down there to see what Mr. Williams had done, and he told me to stop complaining and just fix it. Due to me having to complete what should have been done that night, my schedule was thrown off. The windows were holding up the truck because they are loaded according to the customer stopping location. It was hard but I got it done, but due to the rush they had mixed all the blocks together.

I told the catcher to use one block until the end of the day, and I would straighten them out. Mr. Todd Reed went back and told Mr. Steve Brush that I had no blocks in the glass, but every buggy had blocks in them, although it was only one. We ran over thirteen hundred panels, and only two panels broke. There have been more than that broken with two blocks in the glass. When Mr. Brush got to the department, he said, "George, what did I tell you about those blocks in the glass? I told him that he told me to put two blocks in the glass, but "I told you that was Mr. Williams's glass that he ran from last night and you said okay and then went back to your office." The next thing I knew, he came back and said, "You're fired."

Mr. Peter Atkinson went up front and came back and told me, "George, they demoted you," and I asked why. He said, "Because you did not have blocks in the glass." I told him, "I do have blocks in the glass. I just don't have two blocks in there, and that was due to the mess that Mr. Williams left from last night." He said, "I know I told you to watch yourself," and then I told him, "Peter, it wouldn't matter. I was dammed if I do and dammed if I didn't, because if I would have shut the department down for two hours and not got the loads complete, that would have been blamed on me also. Todd and Steve too, know that the mess was caused by the night shift and it was their fault for not running that glass."

This is what the blocks looked like that I was using to separate the Swiggle glass on the buggies that had to come through the oven where the glass catchers were handling the finished insulated panel. They were long and short and all mixed up together like the ones you will see in this photo. As you can see the photo on page twenty five eighty, percent of those blocks were cut in different lengths. Therefore you couldn't use two of them to support the glass. Mr. Atkinson was aware of that because we discussed the situation concerning the blocks earlier. When I could use two blocks I did. Everybody knew what the situation was concerning this problem and many more just like them, but nothing was done because it was done by the night shift. I didn't know why Mr. Reed and Mr. Brush continued to blame me for all the night shift mistakes and not hold them accountable for not following the rules and regulations that were given to him by Mr. Todd Reed and Mr. Peter Atkinson.

The next thing I knew I was demoted from supervisor. No one could tell me why. Ms. LaShawyna Robinson was promoted to supervisor over the 255/165 Swiggle glass house, and she didn't even know how to read a tape measure, not to mention her experience and attitude. Mr. Peter Atkinson, Mr. Steve Brush, Mr. Todd Reed, and Mr. Lee Wilson all knew she had an attitude problem because they all had dealt with her in the past. All the higher management knew I shouldn't have ever been demoted or left in that department working under the leadership of Ms. LaShawnya Robinson. They all knew that I should have been immediately transferred to another department.

Mr. Reed wanted me to stay in order to be harassed by Ms. Robinson, and she did harass me. She was supervisor for only three days before I took my complaint to Mr. Peter Atkinson and told him that if Ms. Robinson didn't stop harassing me I was going to the office to file a complaint against her. I knew even though she was the supervisor, Mr. Lee Wilson didn't have any love for her either due to her attitude and her past misconduct with the company's rules and regulations. Mr. Peter Atkinson told me that he would talk to her about her attitude. After he talked to her, the harassment stopped.

Ms. Robinson brought an order to me and asked me what went there, and I told her that she was asking the wrong person. I told her that she needed to go to the office and ask the scheduling department that question. She said, "George, you need to stop acting. You know what goes there." I replied and told her that I was a topper. She told Mr. Atkinson that I wouldn't help her. He came to me and said, "George, I know they didn't do you right, but you need to cooperate." I asked him what he meant. He said it again, "You need to cooperate," and I asked him, "Am I not doing my job?" He said, "Yes, but you know what I mean." I told him as long as I was doing my job, there shouldn't be a problem.

No more than a couple weeks later, Mr. Peter Atkinson resigned from the company. Two days later, the harassment started again. They had hundreds of scratched grid bars, and I was taking them out due to scratches. Ms. Robinson asked what I was doing, and I told her that I was taking out the scratched grid bars so that they could redo them. She said I was just trying to slow down the line. I told her that she was the supervisor. I told her that I was not going to be held responsible for scratched grid bars when I told her that they weren't any good. She snatched them and took them back to the grid table for the grid people to remake them.

Mr. David J. Robinson said, "George, why don't you stop trying to help that fool. You see she doesn't want your help." I told him I just couldn't see sending those customers all these scratched up grid bars. Mr. Robinson said, "You see, I haven't said anything to her; she's the one who has to answer to this." I told Mr. Robinson, "Well, I can tell you one thing. When they start pulling these windows out of the warehouse and see all of those scratches, they are going to have a fit." I said that MI would pay the cost for sending out those bad products, and just as I said, it happened.

Mr. Reed called the department up to the meeting room and talked about how the customers were complaining about scratches and touch up paint. I personally blamed Mr. Brush, Mr. Reed, and Mr. Wilson, because when you allow someone leadership over something that they don't even have a clue about what they're doing and understand the importance of good quality, you're automatically facing a losing battle. You never achieve success by placing the wrong people into positions because of personal reasons. They have to be able to perform the task that's set before them. God knows they have set many before me to fail, but I achieved them all. What they did not understand is that situations can't change or stop a special gift that a person has. You have to make adjustments to the situations, and I had to do it with the lack of tools to work with, which is impossible for most people.

After all the things I achieved as a supervisor, it didn't account for anything but hardship within the company. My superiors used other employees and supervisors to attack me when we should have been working together in unity to make it better. The only thing that Mr. Steve Brush could say negative about me was, "George Brown has five racks of miscellaneous glass sitting around the glass cutting area." He failed to include that I said that those racks were from the prior night, which the night shift had made, because as far as my performance, cleanness, organization, and ability he couldn't say anything negative. When you look back over my record as an employee at MI Home Product Inc., you won't find any kind of warnings or written ones concerning my performance nor my ability, and he knew it.

That is why I was the only one he had recommended to go and take the management seminar courses, which were held in Millersburg, Pennsylvania in the year 1998. He recognized the ability that I had as a leader in the production department to make things happen for the benefit of the company and unifying the customers with the quality of the products that they were buying from MI Home Product Inc. This is the statement that he made in his own words, which was told to me but not directly. It was classified, as my department knew that it was done by the night shift supervisor and his crew. At this time, it was the responsibility of Mr. Jimmy Williams and his employees and not mine, according to Mr. Reed. He told me not to worry about what the night shift did at night anyway because that's Mr. Jimmy Williams's shift. But every time something happened on his shift, still Mr. Brush and Mr. Reed pointed their fingers at me for Mr. Williams's wrongdoing.

= 6/30/00

Peter,

Make Sure we Address Clean up
this weekend - Problem Areas -
① Glass Rack in front of joes glass house
② Specialty Frame Area
③ George Brown has 5 racks of Miscl.
glass Sitting around glass Cutter area.
I spoke to him about this yesterday -
NEEDS to get cleaned up and not let
it get in this position again.

CC TODD

Thanks

Steve Brush
General Manager

336 Magnolia Industrial Park • P.O. Box 1038 • Millen, GA 30442 • (912) 982-4330 Ext. 211

Because of the action that Mr. Steve Brush the plant manager and Mr. Todd Reed took, by demoting Mr. Brown it cost the company over a million dollars. They kept trying to cover it up by finger pointing, but I knew at the end somebody would have to be held accountable sooner or later. I knew that one could only do wrong for so long. It would have to end somewhere. You would have to wonder to yourself, how could a company be doing so well and then immediately start going downhill? It's when one allows personal feelings to get in the way of making a business decision, instead of doing what's right; he ends up doing that which is wrong.

After I was demoted in July 2000, that wasn't good enough for Mr. Reed. He started back harassing me through Ms. LaShawyna Robinson, and she didn't have enough sense to hide it. In the beginning of her harassment statement or acts, she would always say, "Todd told me to tell you this," or "Todd told me to tell you that." If Mr. Reed knew she didn't have the ability to do the job, then why did he give her the job? Mr. Reed realized after I wouldn't help her out that he had made a big mistake, but instead of sucking up his pride and doing the right thing, he allowed it to continue on. Ms. Robinson continued to cost the company money due to the materials that she was messing up. It had gotten to the point that she was messing up so bad that he brought in Mr. Jimmy Williams from the night shift in order to help her and put Mr. Chris Reese over the night shift. That didn't work either, because neither one of them had anyone to tell them step by step what it was that they needed to do.

Mr. Steve Brush and Mr. Todd Reed had failed to realize that the only time the night shift had any success was when it was under my authority and instruction. Ms. LaShawyna Robinson continued her harassment until I had gotten tired of it. I went to Mr. Lee Wilson and told him about the harassment that was going on from the supervisor that Mr. Reed had placed over the Swiggle glass house department, which was Ms. Robinson. I requested to be transferred to the glass cutting department. I didn't have any business working under an employee who had worked under me anyway. Due unto her attitude and past history, Mr. Lee Wilson agreed and said to let him talk to Mr. Reed. In a couple of days, Mr. Todd Reed came down to the department and told me, "George, you can go to the glass cutting department tomorrow. You have been transferred down there." I told him okay.

Mr. Reed stayed down there trying to help Ms. Robinson straighten out the 255/165 Swiggle glass house, because it was so disorganized and out of control. I asked Mr. Reed what he wanted me to do, and he told me to cut glass. Mr. Reed told Ms. Robinson to "give George the orders that you want cut," and Mr. Reed was standing right there when she gave me those orders that she wanted me to cut. I cut those orders until it was time for us to get off, and the second shift came in and picked up where I left off. The next day when I came in and reported to the glass cutting department, after about an hour and a half, Ms. Robinson came down there and said, "George, I need you to come to the line and cut an order." I told her that I no longer worked under her. I said that I worked in the glass cutting department, so if she wanted something cut, to bring the order down there and we would cut it for her. She shouted out, "I'm going to write you up." Then the next thing I knew, I was going to the office because Ms. Robinson came back and told me that Mr. Reed wanted to see me.

It was not Ms. Robinson because she didn't know how. It was Mr. Reed writing me up for refusing to follow the supervisor's instruction. The problem was that she was no longer my supervisor at this time; Mr. Joseph Scroggins was. In order to get me she had to go through him. So I asked Mr. Reed where he got that information. He asked, "Did you cut this order?" I told him, "No, you told Ms. Robinson to give me those orders the way she wanted me to cut them and you were standing right there when she gave them to me." I told him that I started cutting the orders in the order that she gave them to me. The order that he had and the one that I was cutting on were left for the night shift glasscutter to finish up.

Mr. Reed just looked at me and said, "Sign here." I told Mr. Reed that I wasn't going to sign anything that I was not responsible for doing. Mr. Reed got mad and shouted at me, "George, you are suspended." Mr. Lee Wilson overheard this and slammed the phone down. He jumped up and walked out and slammed the door behind him, because he was upset over the situation. Mr. Wilson knew the attitude and the incidents that he already encountered with Ms. Robinson. I never had a write up for anything for over seven years at the time, and Ms. Robinson had about a dozen write-ups.

After Mr. Wilson came back in, I (Mr. Brown) told him that I wanted to file a harassment claim against Ms. LaShawyna Robinson. Mr. Wilson told me to go home and type it up and bring it back tomorrow. I told Mr. Wilson that I wasn't going to sign something that I didn't do. He said, "Just sign it and write in your side of the story," and I did. The acting supervisor or the human resource manager didn't write up the disciplinary report, but the assistant plant manager Mr. Todd Reed did. My question is why would an assistant plant manager go out of his way to do something for a young black female when there is a human resource manager to handle situations like that, and then only give me a four-hour suspension? That wasn't even written in the company policy handbook, but Mr. Reed made up something in order to please Ms. Robinson. I couldn't understand why a businessman would go through all of this for a person like Ms. Robinson (unless it was something personal).

After I went home, according to Mr. Charlie Brown, Mr. Reed came down to the glass cutting department and told him if George Brown did anything wrong to let him know and he would be fired. Several weeks later, an employee overheard a conversation between Mr. Todd Reed and Ms. LaShawyna Robinson in the front office. She was telling him that the people on the line weren't doing any production because of George Brown, and Mr. Reed told her that she must stop blaming George for what's happening on her line, because he wasn't even back there now. Mr. Reed realized that he had a big problem, and Ms. Robinson also realized that she had made a big mistake harassing me on her line because I was the only one who could help her. Mr. Reed continued to allow MI Home Product Inc. to be misused by people who didn't have the experience to be in a leadership position, which resulted in causing hundreds of thousands of dollars to be a lost from the company every time Mr. Reed placed an inexperienced person as a supervisor. This was done about six times, which resulted in over a million dollars lost to the company overall, for the hatred of one man.

Go back into the past and check the records from the time that I took the supervisor position from the year 1995 up to July 2000. I had just begun to make big changes in the Millen plant. My goal was to make MI Home Product Inc. stand out in the world. The last thing I helped them accomplish in 2000 was to achieve the first six-million-dollars benchmark. After July 2000, you will find that they were losing money because of one bad judgment call that was approved by Mr. Steve Brush. Instead of demoting me, I should have received a promotion to production manager, because I was the one who was keeping the flow of production going. I helped other supervisors achieve their production, and I helped with the ordering of their supplies.

Mr. Steve Brush called me many times from my department to help other glass houses achieve their production. I would never forget the time when Mr. Brush called me to Mr. Alphonzo Sapp's department. Once I got over there, he said unto me, "If you want to save your friend's job, you had better straighten this mess out, or his ass will be fired." I asked him what was wrong, and he said to me, "Everything." To me it wasn't about Mr. Sapp's job or Mr. Brush, but the company that I worked for.

I called all of the employees together because they all were upset and frustrated, which caused them to be confused in what they were doing. I asked each operating section what they were doing and where they were with their orders. They told me, and in less than an hour production was back on track. Everyone had peace of mind. Mr. Sapp came in about two hours later. I talked with him about the condition of his department, and I told him where we were with production. I then went back to my department.

What most supervisors fail to realize is that it is very important to teach the employees in their department all functions of the job. Then, in the event something happens to the supervisor, the department can continue running. Most supervisors won't do that because of fear of losing their position. They think that they will be replaced. It's much easier to supervise a department when all of the employees are properly trained and you can leave the department and don't have to worry about things going wrong. Even if that happened, it would be a loss to the company because a person with that kind of skill is hard to come by when there's one who can make everyone around him or her good.

I continued to work as a glasscutter, but that still wasn't enough for Mr. Reed. After he had me demoted. In December 2000, he also had my wife laid off, even though she had years of experience. Everybody in that department had fewer years of service than she had. Instead of letting her stay or sending her to another department, Mr. Lee Wilson decided that he wouldn't follow the company's employee manual. During my time as a supervisor, I wanted to lay off an employee who had less experience than another employee. Mr. Wilson told me that we had to go by the length of service with the company. I had to lay off a good worker instead of dead weight who had been written up before, but it didn't hurt the function of my production, because I placed her in a non-demanding position.

As time went by, Mr. Todd Reed wanted to start up the GED Optimizer glass cutting machine, so he decided to send Mr. Joseph Scroggins and Mr. Charlie Brown to a GED Optimizer operational seminar in order to learn how to operate the machine. I could understand why he was sending Mr. Charlie Brown to the seminar in order to learn how to operate the machine, but I couldn't understand why he would want to waste the company's money on sending Mr. Joseph Scroggins. He was a supervisor. He wouldn't be the one operating the Optimizer due to the fact that he had a department to run.

When they came back, they were excited. When it came time to operate the Optimizer machine, the only thing Mr. Charlie Brown remembered was how to turn on the power. The only thing Mr. Joseph Scroggins knew was how to make it cut one piece of glass at a time and the glass had to be the same size. Mr. Scroggins said the instructor told him that whatever he cut, he would have to cut the whole unit the same size. In order to cut different sizes, the machine would have to be programmed on a disk by the scheduling department. The scheduling department started downloading the cutting sizes on the disk the wrong way. When the machine cut it, we had to throw a lot of glass away, because it was programmed wrong on the disk. They ordered new computers and had them installed. They were supposed to have them programmed with the proper cut size and thickness, but the thickness was all wrong. It was giving out the wrong thickness of glass thickness dsb when it should have been ssb, and 3/16 when it should have been dsb.

Due to this error, it was causing the company to lose money. If the customer hadn't ordered that thickness of glass, they didn't have to pay for it. When I brought it to Mr. Reed's attention, he told me not to worry about that. He said that I was to cut what the order called for. I told him, sure, no problem. This is what the 255/165 Swiggle glass house looked like after I was demoted from that department. No one said anything about what was going on, because no one had a solution. You will see that there are no blocks in this glass. Because of their pride, they wouldn't say they made a mistake and promote me back to a supervisor. I could have put that glass department back on track to produce the insulated glass units that the window lines needed in order to achieve their windows production in a timely manner in order to be loaded by shipping.

This picture will show that for me not having two blocks in the glass wasn't their reason for demoting me. If that was the reason for my demotion, then why weren't the supervisors who ran this glass demoted or written up? I can tell you why. Because blocks weren't the issue to start off with. That was the only thing that they could come up with in order to demote me from supervisor. They didn't care how much money it would cost the company, but why should they care? It wasn't their money. I'll tell you why. If the company entrusted them to run their company and protect their interests, they should do so regardless of their personal reasons. They should have had the best interests of MI Home Production Inc., because they are the ones who trusted Mr. Brush and Mr. Reed to make sure that their materials were used properly for the company's benefit.

This picture will show how much scrap glass was wasted daily—not weekly. This wasn't counting the wasted grid bars that were thrown away with the glass. All of this resulted in a continual loss to the company. Instead of solving the problems, all they wanted to do was point fingers. What was even more disturbing Mr. Pete DeSoto fell for it. These pictures will show what Mr. Brush and Mr. Reed tried to hide. I knew that it would come out into the open. The company buys the materials, and if they aren't sold and aren't in the inventory at the end of the year, where does the money that they paid for the materials go? I knew that if they came forward now or later (at the end of the year), it would all show up. It was all because of poor management by the ones whom Mr. DeSoto placed in charge of running his company.

Mr. Brush was a good manager until he allowed friendship to get in the way of his better judgment. His sense of direction began to fall apart for him. Mr. Brush had so many problems happening to him at one time, until he couldn't regain his focus on what he was doing. One thing is for sure—Mr. Reed knew what was happening at the time. He undermined Mr. Brush, knowing that his leadership would collapse. I was removed from my position. Mr. Brush fell for it, and it cost him his job. Mr. Reed was standing right there waiting for it, and I can assure you Mr. Brush realizes that now.

Here are some more pictures in order to get a clear understanding of what was going on in the plant during that time of bad decision making by Mr. Steve Brush and Mr. Todd Reed.

This is glass from today, but not the only harper that was dumped on a daily basis. You must realize this went on through six different supervisors leaders (in title only). They didn't have the experience for the job. It hurt me to see the department I turned into being the number one unit per man hour (which is in the True Seal magazine) turn out like this when it was doing so well under my leadership. Someone would have to wonder what in the world went wrong with MI Home Inc. in Millen, Georgia. It was on a fast track of becoming number one, and now it looked as if it was just starting operations in production.

The waste of glass and metal materials didn't have a short duration. It was over a year's time with over two million dollars in losses to the company. All of this happened because of the demotion of George Brown. I was the one that kept the other departments straightened out. I would order their materials and train them how to order their own materials even after I was demoted. I still had to help them order their materials until they learned how to order on their own. Mr. Reed knew this, and that's why I was shocked to hear that I was demoted. The entire plant was shocked to hear that I was demoted, because they knew that I was the one who had production running like it was.

Mr. A.D. Pierce, a supervisor at Bell Crest Homes (a plant next door), said to me, "George, you must be the head man at that plant. I hear your name called all the time." The reason for that is I had to solve a lot of problems that arose from time to time within the plant.

Here are some more pictures in order to show what was happening after my demotion in July 2000. Mr. Reed was the one who led to this disaster. It was his own greed and deceit against MI and Mr. Steve Brush because he wanted to be over the company.

This is a continuation of materials being wasted by the ones who Mr. Reed allowed to be in charge of the 255/165 Swiggle glass house.

Insulated and raw glass were thrown away due to numerous errors from both the department itself and from the scheduling department. When I was a supervisor, I had to go back to the office on many occasions to have the order rechecked due to mistakes made on the order. I never liked doing the same thing twice, because it hinders production within the department, which can result in overtime. I didn't believe in overtime unless it was necessary. I view overtime as a loss to the company. It also increases the risk of employees getting injuries and having to be out from work for a long period of time, costing the plant even more money along with the excessive waste of materials.

This is the following day. This is what was happening every day for over a month. Then it went to two or three times a week compared to zero to one time per week when I was in charge of that department. When I was supervisor over 255/165 glass department, I asked the True Seal representatives how many units were supposed to break a day. He told me he didn't know. I said, "You don't know?" He said it depended on the temperature. It would have to be a certain degree and stay at the same degree all the time, and the temperature varies in the South a lot, unlike the North. The people are the same. A good supervisor has to adjust the people unto the situation at hand, and this makes it difficult for most of the supervisors in the South. They think that people will automatically know what and how to do it.

I compare employees to football. When they get new players, they don't change the coach's style. The players adapt to their style of playing by being trained to do so. There are more pictures to verify what I'm saying about Mr. Todd Reed. Everything I have said is true and factual from the things that I have witnessed. I was hoping that someone would step up and say something about the situations that were going on in the plant due unto Mr. Reed and the ones he used to help him.

It isn't acceptable for a supervisor to have finished panels stacked on a cart like this, nor are there blocks in between the glass in order to decrease the pressure on the glass to keep it from sticking together. Where is the leadership that was held responsible for this? Who will be held accountable? Mr. Reed would rather see MI go down to nothing than to admit his faults, which were due to pride, greed, and self-gain.

A person with an attitude like that cannot work as a team player. There would always be frustration and deception in the midst of the team, and there wouldn't be anything done when working in a bad environment setting. This sort of problem would be caused by someone who is supposed to be showing leadership to the supervisors. The supervisors are supposed to pass it to all the employees to let them know we all are one with one goal in mind, and that is 100 percent complete, 100 percent shipped, and 100 percent on time. That was the MI slogan, and that's what we stood behind.

When I was demoted in July 2000, Mr. Steve Brush and Mr. Todd Reed said it was because of boards not being placed in the glass. They had forgotten who it was that got MI to the place it was. You can go back and check my production record from 1995 to July 2000 and see for yourself how I changed the status of MI Home Product Inc. and what it lost after the month of July. This is a continuation of how they stacked glass on the buggies and continued to have unnecessary breakage of panel after panel due to the lack of leadership and the lack of concern for the company. This is the way things continued to be, and there still aren't any blocks in all of the glass. It was never about blocks or anything else, as far as my production and finished products were concerned. It was about destroying George Brown no matter what the cost would be to the company, as long as Mr. Reed was satisfied that I was to be demoted from a supervisor position, but he still wasn't satisfied.

He tried to cause me financial hardship by having my salary reduced. As time continued on, he demoted Mr. Rick Lineberry, but he didn't reduce his pay other than him not receiving his bonuses. He was no longer a supervisor. He worked in the supply room handing out materials to the supervisors for their lines in order to run production. They continued to pay him until he was no longer with the company.

On buggies after buggies, there weren't any blocks in it at all. This repeated itself daily until Mr. Gary Hetrich started walking the floor himself to witness how the situation had gotten out of control. It was constantly costing the company money, and the plant was a mess. Broken glass and trash were everywhere throughout the plant. Then Mr. Reed started blaming Mr. Bush when he himself was the ringleader. The only thing that Mr. Brush was at fault for was trusting his assistant and not checking things out for himself. If you were to check Mr. Brush's record at MI Home Product Inc. in Millen, Georgia, before he made Mr. Reed his assistant, you will find that he had a great record.

When Mr. Reed became general manager, it was about sex and power. My opinion is that's how Ms. LaShawyna Robinson attained her position. She sure didn't have the experience or the knowledge to be in the position that Mr. Reed placed her. What amazed me was the fact that Mr. Lee Wilson knew that, because he had dealt with her on many occasions. He knew what type of person she was. Still he allowed this to go on. I can assure you that Mr. Wilson and I knew that it wasn't in the best interests of the company. He knew that with her being in charge of any line, it would cost the company some money by investing in Ms. Robinson. It happened anyway because Mr. Reed wanted it.

Mr. Brush and Mr. Wilson allowed Mr. Reed to have her as a supervisor. Everybody in the plant knew that Mr. Reed had made a bad decision by choosing her as a supervisor. The employees were saying among themselves that Todd must have lost his mind placing Ms. Robinson as a supervisor. They said that if he didn't put George Brown back over this line it was going to go down. It did go down—fast.

Here's a picture of raw glass that they placed on the buggy any kind of way. This sort of thing could cause injuries.

This buggy of glass had been run through the washer, and it was the wrong size glass. This is against the company policies. The glass is broken, and when someone walks by, it can fall and cut someone. It sat there for days, and nobody said anything. When you stack glass on a buggy like this, it makes it easy to scratch the other glass behind it. They had so much glass like this that had to be thrown away. This is not counting the glass on the back of the oven. This wasn't the only buggy that was done like this one. This was one of the better ones. There have been buggies that had far more glass on it than this one that had to be thrown away.

At one point it had gotten so bad that they stopped weighing the harpers and started dumping the glass into the containers. They didn't want to turn in all that scrap glass to the main office in Pennsylvania, or the scrap metal from the windows or the grid bars, because of the excessive waste. This is a prime example of wasted materials from the leadership that Mr. Reed had placed in charge of overseeing of the company goods.

Mr. Reed tried his best to hide this mess by blaming others, when in fact he's to blame. By not realizing that, at the end of the year, when the main inventory time comes, it would come back to haunt him. He didn't have anybody to blame for his mishandling of the MI Home Product Inc. but himself.

There was a buggy of glass that had been run wrong and could not be used. If you were to take all of the mishaps that resulted in dollars turning bad due to constant waste and turn them into good dollars that could have been used toward purchasing some more materials for the company, this would have put profit back into the company instead of taking profit out of the company.

I wonder who pays for all of the bad glass that isn't used? Who does it hurt? It hurts the employees and the company itself. Due to improper and poor management, they will have to reduce their costs by downsizing the employees and cutting their pay. This is something that the leadership has caused, yet they continue receiving their pay like nothing ever happened. They don't care who gets hurt as long as it's not them. The employees lose their income, health insurance, and independency. Some of them were cut off from their income without any kind of notice, unlike what they want you to do when you get ready to leave. They want you to put in two week's notice in advance.

Fair measure says that when a long-term employee who has been rated above average is given new goals, the employer must help him or her reach those goals. That would include mentoring, sending him or her to training, giving him or her books to read, assigning them a buddy who can coach them, managing more closely than usual, etc. When I was asked to take over the line, I got the opposite. They did everything humanly possible to hinder me from production. They wanted me to be a supervisor, glasscutter, trainer, and lead person, all at the same time. Still I was determined to succeed. It didn't matter whether I succeeded or not. Mr. Reed had his mind already made up about removing me. He failed to realize that he would have to have someone who was just as good as or better at the job than I was. The options that he had to choose from were nowhere close to supervisor material. I was the best man for the job; with me it's a gift, and that's something that can't be given or taken away. It doesn't matter how much you like a person, you cannot make them into something that they are not. It's a good thing to help people, but one must understand that everyone is not born to be a leader, and Ms. Robinson wasn't born to be a leader. After Mr. Reed placed her as supervisor, it was too late. She wasn't supervisor material, and all the help in the world couldn't change her into a leader. She didn't like to follow instructions.

This is part of the reason the customers received scratched dirty grids. The supervisor allowed the grid assembly employees to pile them up on the table and put them on the dirty floor. When you stack grids on the table like this (metal on metal), it scratches the paint off some of those grids if not all of them. This was because of the lack of concern for the company property by the leadership. This should have been their number one concern, but it didn't matter to them as long as they continued to receive their salary biweekly from the company.

This is what they call being organized, and still you won't find any blocks in this glass. Why anyone wasn't held accountable for this? I did more for the company than any supervisor that works or worked at MI Home Product Inc., and I didn't get a promotion or recognition for all the hard work that I put in. But I did get a demotion by Mr. Todd Reed, who didn't think about the company interests and the losses they would take.

Units like this being thrown away every day cannot be a benefit unto the company. Mr. Reed stood by and watched units like this being thrown away for scrap. He still refused to do what he knew could fix the problem.

You cannot control the temperature with the door open, which contributed to some of the bad panels. Keeping the door open also causes dirt to get on the inside of the glass. When the door opens, loose trash blows around in the air. The panels are thrown away due to the trash that has gotten in between the glass panels, causing the glass to be dirty.

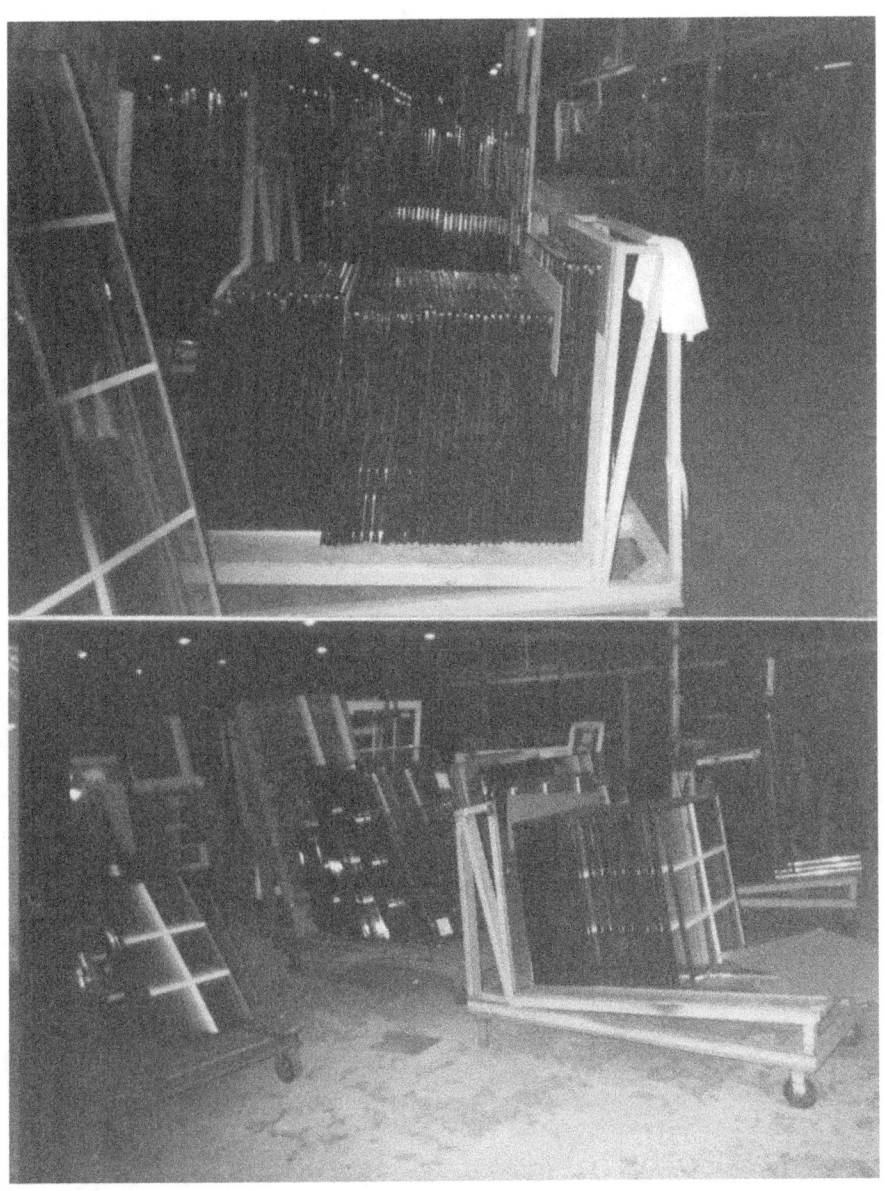

There still aren't any blocks in between these glass panels, and no date stamped on them. I guess that I was the only one who had to make a miracle happen. Harassing a person constantly goes farther than race and sex.

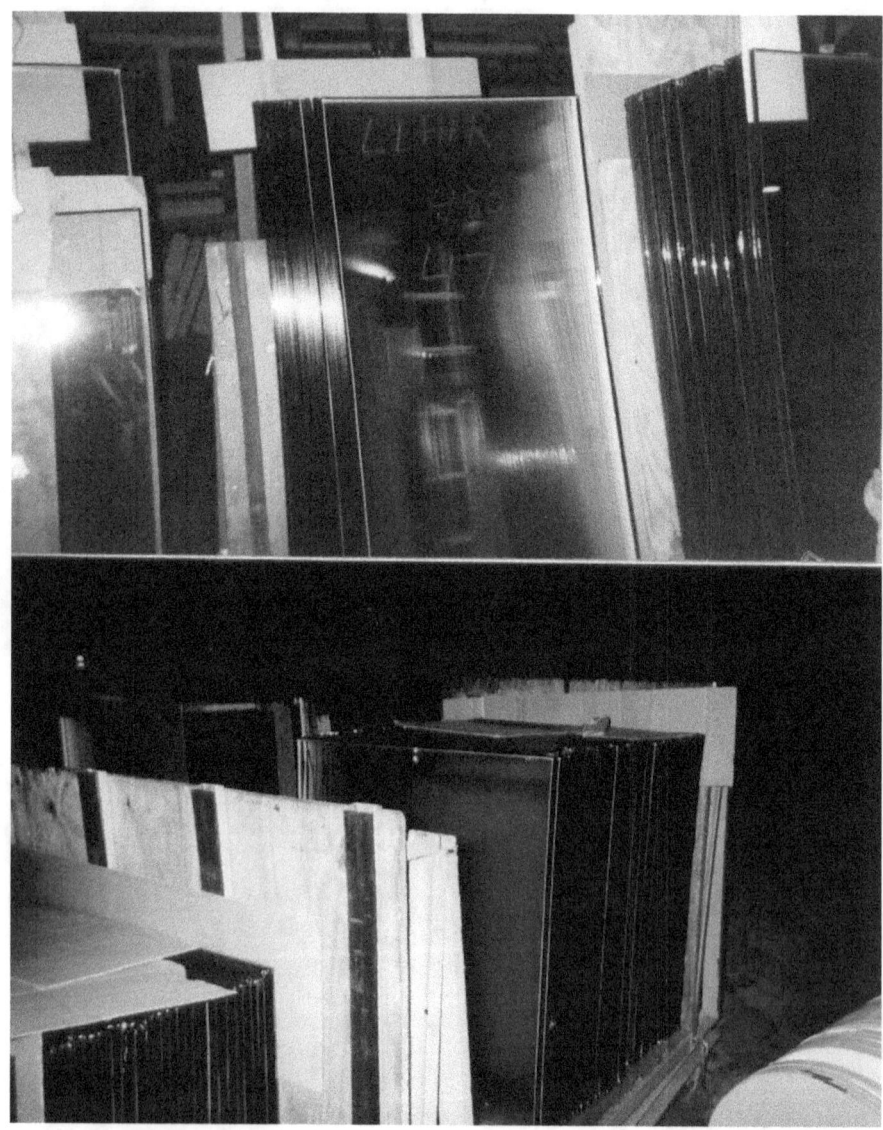

It really didn't make any sense to me why they would prefer to take me down without a cause and watch MI Home lose hundreds of thousands of dollars. I understand what Mr. Reed's reason was. I did not understand Mr. Brush, other than being deceived by a friend who was seeking his job no matter what the cost to MI Home Product Inc. or anyone else.

These pictures do not lie; this was the only way that I could tell my story and have proof to back it up. The law is one-sided when it comes to the wealthy. You take Mr. Chad Oglesby, who the supervisor over the 450 window line and found out that he couldn't handle it. Mr. Reed then decided to make him a supervisor over one employee sweeping the floor. He paid him a supervisor's salary for a while, until he had no other choice but to put him on a line and let him work or let him go. Mr. Oglesby refused to work on a line under someone, so he quit. My main point is why would you waste company money on something like this? There was no one who attempted to stop Mr. Reed from making all of these incompetent decisions.

This plant went on looking like this for days, and it seem to bother nobody but Mr. Gary Hetrick and me. Mr. Hetrick didn't want to go against his associates for me, but he should have been thinking about the benefit of the company instead of his associates.

From 1994 to 2000, I accomplished a lot for MI Home Product Inc. I even achieved operation of the GED Optimizer and never went to the seminar for it, unlike my co-workers who did attend the Optimizer seminar and couldn't operate it. Ms. Lucy Bowers came into the production area to test a disk onto which she'd downloaded some cut sizes. She wanted to see if the Optimizer would cut it. She called Mr. Charlie Brown over to operate it. The only thing he could do was turn the power on. He told her that she needed to "get George," because I knew more about it than he did. Ms. Bowers called me over to the Optimizer to start it up, and it cut the sizes she had downloaded onto the disk. She told me that she would be right back. I said okay. She went back into the scheduling department and came back an hour later with Mr. Kelly Islam to show him how the GED Optimizer works. When they got to the machine, she called for someone to come over there. Mr. Charlie Brown went over there, and she told him to get George Brown. I went over to see what she wanted. She told me to show Mr. Islam how the Optimizer works. I took the Optimizer through a process of steps in order to demonstrate how it operates, and he said, "Okay, thank you, George."

They went back to the office to prepare for the Optimizer cutting schedule. After they decided to go ahead with the Optimizer operation, Mr. Reed decided that it wasn't in the best interests of the company to place Mr. Charlie Brown in charge of operating the machine. When I asked them questions concerning the machine, no one could tell me anything. Yet they could tell me what they wanted me to cut with it. I told Mr. Reed that I needed some information about the Optimizer. He told me to talk to Mr. Scroggins about it. I called Mr. Scroggins and asked him about the Optimizer. He told me that he didn't know that much about the Optimizer. He said that I knew more about it than he did. They had told him that due to the age of the Optimizer, it couldn't cut but one size at a time. He said that whatever I programmed in there for it to cut manually, it cuts the whole sheet that size. He told me that Lucy would have to download the order on a disk for me. I said, "Okay, thank you, but that wasn't any help. I already knew that."

I had problems when a piece of glass would break; I had to wait too long for the office to reprogram the repairs. I knew if there was a machine that operated automatically, then it would also operate manually. I asked Mr. Kelly Islam if he had an operating manual. He said yes. I then asked him if I could take it home and study it. Every time I asked someone about this Optimizer, no one can tell me anything about it. He said, "Yes, go ahead and take it home." After the day ended, I took the GED Optimizer manual home and began studying it. I had mastered it at the end of the week. I found out that it would cut whatever I wanted to cut as long as it was within the cut length of the glass in which it would be cut from. Whether it's two pieces or twenty pieces, it didn't matter.

I began to train Mr. Homer Hendrix how to manually set up different cuts out of one sheet. Mr. Scroggins saw me cutting multiple sizes. He asked me how I did that. He said that at the seminar they told him that the machine would only cut one piece of glass at a time. I told him if they told him that, they didn't know what they were talking about, because this machine will cut whatever you want it to cut. We then began full production on the machine. Mr. Reed realized that I knew what I was doing. Mr. Charlie Brown continued operating on the manual cutting table because he couldn't operate the Optimizer.

After I taught Mr. Hendrix how to operate the Optimizer, the harassments started back up again. Mr. Scroggins started sending me to the Swiggle glass houses trying to degrade my pay. I asked him what his problem was. He said, "What do you mean?" I told him that I couldn't be going to the Swiggle glass houses all the time, because there were three people there and you are supposed to switch out, not send the same person. He was doing just that until Mr. Charlie Brown started complaining about going to the Swiggle glass houses, and Mr. Scroggins started switching out Mr. Hendrix and me. He all of a sudden started harassing me every time somebody was out. He wanted to send me to take their place to degrade my pay. The company policy was that you would have to receive equal pay to what you were making.

When I came in the next morning, he wanted me to go to the Swiggle glass house. I told him that I wanted to see Mr. Jerry Jacob. He said he wouldn't come in until eight o'clock. At this time, he was the production manager. When he did come over, I told Mr. Jacob that Mr. Scroggins keep sending me from department to department trying to degrade my pay. It wasn't right. He said, "George, there's nothing that I can do; you will have to go wherever Mr. Scroggins sends you." I told him that I wanted to talk with Mr. Wilson, and he told me okay. He called Mr. Scroggins and told him to put Mr. Alphonzo

Sapp back there. When Mr. Sapp came over, I went and talked to Mr. Wilson and I told him that Mr. Scroggins was trying to degrade my pay by sending me from department to department. I told him that he needed to balance it out by sending everyone, or I would take what I made over there and bring it back here and divide it three ways. Mr. Wilson said, "Let me talk to Mr. Jacob and Mr. Scroggins." I said okay. After Mr. Wilson talked to them, it stopped for a while. He then started switching us out like he should have done to start off with. One day Mr. Bran Sitter came by, and I asked him why we couldn't put our piece rates together when one of us is sent to another department to work. He said, "You can if everyone agrees with it, that's what we did in Pennsylvania. But you will need to ask Mr. Kelly Islam." I told him to tell him that I needed to see him.

When Mr. Islam came to the department, I told him about the situation that we were having. I told him that we wanted to add our piece rate together and divide it three ways. Everyone was there when the conversation was going on, and everyone agreed to it. Mr. Islam approved it. Everything went along fine for a while, until Mr. Charlie Brown decided that he wanted to work over in the Swiggle glass house and get paid out of what we done in the glass cutting department. I told Mr. Scroggins that when he told us that was it for today, then that's it. If Mr. Charlie Brown wanted to work over with him, then he should pay him out of the Swiggle glass house. I told him that we could all stay there together or he could pay him for maintenance; but he couldn't pay him out of something that was already done.

Mr. Charlie Brown started leaving the plant while Mr. Hendrix and I were still working. He would come back, and Mr. Scroggins would pay him for the whole day. He did that for several months. Mr. Alphonzo Sapp was also doing the same thing for years. Mr. Scroggins paid him for the whole day, and there wasn't anything said. He stayed out and was late many times. Mr. Hendrix started doing it also, and again there wasn't anything done. They would leave and go downtown to cash their check during the working hours, and there wasn't anything done about that either.

As time continued on, Mr. Scroggins called us and told us that Mr. Todd Reed told him to take three hours from everybody and pay the lead people of the Swiggle glass houses. I told him that he must be crazy if he thought for a moment that I would pay someone who hasn't done anything for me, and he said, "Well whether you like it or not, that what's going to happen." I told him to go ahead and do it, and I'd take a warrant out on him and Todd. I asked him if he knew that it was theft by taking money, and the law calls that a crime. Mr. Reed had already told Mr. Scroggins to do it to the Swiggle houses for Mr. Alphonzo Sapp. He had paid Mr. Sapp for over a year, 50 percent from the 255/165 Swiggle glass house. He should not have been paid eight hours a day or fourteen hours per day. He didn't do anything for the 255/165 Swiggle glass house, and hardly anything for the other glass dept, instead of MI Home Product Inc. paying Mr. Sapp. They made the employees pay him from their earnings for over a year, and that's nothing but a crime. How can a company hire an employee and then want the employees to pay him for working for MI Home Product Inc.? After they realized that they could get by with it, they wanted to add Mr. Eric Gibson in their pay. Mr. Reed and Mr. Scroggins decided that they could steal from the employees, because they were not afraid of losing their jobs. No one was doing anything about it anyway, so they felt comfortable doing it.

Mr. Lee Wilson allowed this to go on. MI Home Product Inc. owed those employees back pay for almost two years of money that they stole from them and gave to other employees who weren't helping them at all. They had the authority to do so. There are many companies out there that may have lawsuits, but is it their fault, or is it MI Home Product Inc. fault? They sold them materials that weren't qualified for passing inspection, but were passed through because of the outer appearance due unto the quality of the glass panels.

They cut back on the material. When we used to purchase materials from Allmetal Inc., you could take a twelve-feet grid bar that was already prefabricated and hold it up, and it would stand up. When they stopped buying from Allmetal Inc. and started buying from their own company, you could stand that same size grid bar up and it would bend over. Not only was the grid-bar material weaker but also the doors. The window material was weaker and the glass thickness wasn't within the proper standard of thickness, which made the product much weaker, especially in many of Lowe's and the State of Florida window and products. If they went back to inspect some of their products that their associates and the consumers complained about, they would find out that a lot of those complaints were not their responsibility, but the material that they purchased through MI Home Product Inc.

I was demoted. My wife was laid off. I was harassed, and through all of that Mr. Reed still wasn't satisfied. I was being demoted for no reason at all on my part in 2000. In 2003, I was laid off working with Mr. Homer Hendrix and Mr. Charlie Brown in the Glass cutting department. My recorded absentees and company misconduct was much better than theirs. Mr. Scroggins was my supervisor at this time. He, Mr. Reed, or Mr. Jacobs did not come to me. They were the ones over me. They sent Mr. Richard Morris to tell me that Mr. Lee Wilson wanted to see me. When I got to his office, Mr. Wilson said, "Come on in, George." He said, "I hate that it has come to this but due to September 11, I'm going to lay you off." I asked Mr. Wilson what this was. I had a better record than anybody in that department. There had to be more to it than that. Mr. Wilson said, "George, you know me better than that." I told him I thought I did. They laid me off and put an employee there who didn't have any experience in cutting.

I always believed that this incident stemmed off of an incident that happened the latter part of 2002. Mr. Reed had tried to falsely accuse me of cheating on the piece rate. I told him that I didn't do piece rate sheets. He asked me who did them. I told him that Mr. Hendrix and Mr. Sapp did them. He then dropped the whole matter. I felt that if something were wrong with the piece rate sheet, then the ones who did them should have been held accountable for it, but because it wasn't me, he dropped the whole conversation. I knew that I would never get fired for any misconduct because I always believe in following the company rules and regulations.

Mr. Reed told Mr. Scroggins that he didn't want us to cut anything without paperwork. I didn't have a problem with that, because I always prefer to have paperwork to back up what I cut so that there isn't any misunderstanding with the instructions. Mr. Prescott came over and wanted some glass cut without any paperwork. I told him that we couldn't cut it; he needed to go and see Mr. Scroggins. He became enraged. He went and got Mr. Scroggins and came back. Mr. Scroggins said when Mr. Prescott comes over here for some glass, to cut it. I reminded Mr. Scroggins that he'd just told us that morning that Mr. Reed said not to cut anything without any paperwork. He told us if we did, then we wouldn't get paid for it. I told them if there isn't any paperwork, then I'm not cutting it. He said, "Oh you are going to cut it." I said yes I would with paperwork. He said, "You aren't getting any paperwork, but you're going to cut it." I told him that I wanted to see Mr. Reed. He told me to come on.

We went to his office, but he wasn't there. Ms. Lucy Bowers said he was upstairs with Mr. Mike Jackson. We went upstairs where Mr. Todd Reed, Mr. Mike Jackson (who is the president of all of MI Home Inc.), and also Mr. Steve Landsman were all upstairs together. Mr. Scroggins said, "Todd, George wants to talk to you." I asked him, "Didn't you tell Mr. Scroggins this morning that you didn't want us to cut any glass without any paperwork? You said that if we did, then we would not be getting paid for it." Mr. Reed replied, "Yes, I told him that! You could have cut that glass while you're up here." A rage came over him suddenly, and he shouted out and said, "Why are you up here anyway? I just caught you stealing last week." I told him, "You haven't caught me doing anything, because I don't steal." Mr. Mike Jackson looked at Mr. Reed and shook his head. He asked Mr. Steve Landsman if he had some type of form to order glass on. Mr. Landsman told Mr. Jackson, "Yes, we have some repair tickets that they order glass on." He asked why he couldn't write it up on that.

Mr. Reed was mad ever since that incident, and that's what the layoff was all about. He knew that Mr. Homer Hendrix told him that he was the one who does the piece rates. He continued to say that I was the one who was responsible for the piece rate sheets. I wasn't the acting supervisor. Mr. Joseph Scroggins was. I believe that if any other party should have been blamed, he should have. It was his job to go over the entire piece rate and make sure they were correct. It wasn't any surprise to him. The reason he didn't change it was because of his friend Mr. Alphonzo Sapp. He wanted to make sure that Mr. Sapp was happy with his salary, regardless of whom he was stealing money to give to Mr. Sapp. Whether it was from the company or the employees, it didn't matter to him as long as Mr. Sapp got paid.

I worked in the specialty glass house a whole pay period in order to keep the glass houses running, because Mr. Thomas Pierce was in the hospital. We had to cut the glass for the 255/165 glass, too. Some days we worked from 6:00 a.m. to 11:00 p.m. in order to keep the plant running. We did all of this just to have our money stolen by Mr. Todd Reed. We signed a statement for Mr. Reed to make adjustments. The adjustment I thought he was going to make was to take the extra glass out that Mr. Joseph Scroggins had told Mr. Hendrix to put in for me working in the glass house. He wanted to take the hours I had in the glass house to help build up Mr. Sapp's salary. The bad thing about this was, Mr. Reed knew that.

After my layoff, I wrote a letter to Mr. Mike Jackson and expressed to him the situation. He responded back by saying that the reason for the layoff was reorganizing the plant, and I was to keep in touch with Lee Wilson. I wrote Mr. Jackson back and told him that wasn't the reason they laid me off and put in an employee who didn't know anything about cutting in my place. Mr. Jackson contacted Mr. Wilson, and then they moved the new employee and placed Mr. Alphonzo Sapp over there. He didn't know how to operate the Optimizer either. He had to be taught by Mr. Hendrix, whom I taught. Later on Mr. Wilson was calling the laid off employees back and hiring new employees. He still would not call me back. I contacted Mr. Jackson again and told him about the situation. He made them call me back.

When I went back to the plant, I talked with Mr. Sapp and he didn't like it. He went and told Mr. Scroggins that he had to move me. Mr. Scroggins came over and told me, "George, what are you doing over here?" I told him, "Mr. Wilson told me to come over here and he said, 'I don't need you over here.'" I told him that he needed to go and talk to Mr. Wilson because he was the one who told me to go over there and this was where I was going to stay.

After the next two days, he wanted me to go to the glass house. I told him that as long as it wasn't going to interfere with my pay. He said, "No, you'll make the same pay that Mr. Sapp and Mr. Hendrix make." I said okay. While I was down there, he asked me how I came back out there. I said, "What do you mean?" He said Mr. J.R. Minich called him up to the office and asked him if he had any problem with George Brown coming back, because he didn't have any choice. He had to bring George back. I told him, "No, really Mr. Todd Reed made me lay him off." I didn't have any problem with him, but at this time Mr. Reed was no longer the plant manager of MI Home Product Inc. in Millen, Georgia, due to Mr. Reed's inability to maintain the plant in good operational condition in order to continue MI's standard of operating. Regardless of how Mr. Reed misused the company and the company funds, they still refused to fire him.

I did nothing but contribute to the company in order to make it better. I was terminated for something that I didn't even do. Even Mr. Pete DeSoto wasn't willing to listen to my side of the incident that took place concerning me. I wasn't even there when it started. The people who actually took part in it weren't written up, suspended, or fired. What they fail to tell was when I first went to the P-175 glass department, it was in a mess. They had over two thousands windows out there already in the market that had been sent back. There was no one held accountable. The engineer made all punch sizes wrong on P-175 picture windows, and many of them were shipped to the customers. Who was held accountable for all those picture windows? The scheduling department Incorrectly ordered so much tempered glass; thousands and thousands of dollars were thrown away due to wrong sizes. Who was held accountable for that? There were orders being scheduled out to the floor with numerous mishaps, and the glass was cut and ran through the insulation department and ended up having to be thrown away. Who was held accountable for that?

Mr. Clint Forehand and Mr. Richard Morris were trying to straighten out the P-175 glass house and running all those insulated glass panels incorrectly, which resulted into thousands of dollars being lost. Who was held accountable? When the grid-cutting department, whose supervisor is Mr. James Jackson, cut those 165 series 5/8 white grids wrong with four, six, eight, and nine lite panels, Mr. Steve Landsman and Mr. JR Minich wanted me to help Mr. Landsman separate the good ones from the bad ones. I didn't have anything to do with these, but I was willing to step in and help save the company some money. I tried to save some grids that were cut and made out of bad material. Who was held accountable for that?

Mr. James Prescott Jr. ran hundreds of patio door panels with crooked grids in them, and Mr. Harner and Mr. Minich were going to throw them away. I told them that most of those panels could be used because they were going in mobile homes and not going to be matched up with any windows. That stopped them from throwing all of them away. They didn't know that those panels could be used. They were only a 1/8 to 3/16 of an inch off. They had a few that were a half of an inch off, which had to be thrown away. This resulted in going from hundreds of panels to only thirty panels being thrown away. Who was held accountable for that?

Mr. Johnny Richardson turned over a crate of glass and broke it. He would sometimes run into a crate with the forklift and break up glass. Who is held accountable for it? Or when the specialty glass house runs those special panels wrong almost every day. Who is held accountable for it? None of these employees are new, nor were they trying to learn something new. There are many things that you can blame people for, but the things that the top leadership in the company was trying to blame me for were totally wrong. I have never in my life seen leaders fight against leaders like I have witnessed at MI Home Product Inc. in Millen, Georgia. You don't blame the supervisors for something that the employees do without their supervisor's permission, because if that were the case there wouldn't be any supervisors left to supervise anyone.

After all I'd done for that company, I thought that Mr. Pete DeSoto would have at least listened to both sides of the story and spoken up for the right like Mr. Mike Jackson did, but Mr. DeSoto didn't even have or would not even find the time to give me an answer back on my complaint. I explained to him what had happened. I wrote and told Mr. Pete DeSoto that I didn't feel that I was treated fairly.

Mr. Lynn Harner himself, according to Mr. Lee Wilson, discharged me for something that the employees Mr. Brad and Mr. James Jackson had done while I was on jury duty. He fired me because he said it was my line. I told him, "Yes, it's my line, but I wasn't even here when those grids were cut, punched or put together." There's one thing that I can say; Mr. Pete Desoto cannot deny that the P-175 windows and insulated glass panels were in deep trouble before I was called back to work by Mr. Mike Jackson through Mr. Lee Wilson in June 2003.

When I returned back to work, they had two supervisors trying to run that glass house—Mr. Clint Forehand and Mr. Richard Morris. They were trying their best to get the P-175 glass house going, but they just didn't have the ability to do so. It wasn't that they weren't trying; they could only do what their ability would allow them to do and that just wasn't enough.

Mr. J.R. Minich came to me and told me that he wanted me to go on that line and top until he hired someone. I told him okay. I topped for several weeks, and things didn't seem to get any better. Then one day Mr. Minich came back there to the P-175 glass house line. I told him that I couldn't help him much by topping, but I could help more by running the department. At the time Mr. Minich couldn't receive that. It was the furthest thing from his mind. He didn't want me back to start off with. Mr. Mike Jackson forced them to hire me back, because he knew what they had done was wrong and against MI polices. Mr. Minich didn't have any other choice after the two supervisors he'd put in charge were constantly making mistakes and having to throw away thousands of dollars of insulated panels weekly. He came to and said, "George, I have a man coming in next week; when he gets here I want you to help Clint run the line." I said okay because I knew then it would give me the opportunity to show them what I know and how much I could benefit MI Home Product Inc.

Mr. Clint Forehand was still the supervisor and getting the credit, but he wanted me to run it. After I began to bring the P-175 glass house together, Mr. Minich began to see a big difference. Under my supervision, the line was coming together unlike it had been when the other supervisors were running it. Mr. Minich was very disappointed because he wanted me to fail. I had the experience and ability, so failing was not an option. He tried everything humanly possible to make it happen. After he saw that the P-175 glass house was coming together, he tried everything to make it disorganized. He wouldn't let me work someone in the department. He always wanted to pull a different person from other lines, and then they would have to go back when their supervisor needed them. He would then find someone else. He never would give me anyone who had glass experience. I told Mr. Minich that it was hard to run a line and train different people every day. I told him that he needed to go ahead and hire someone who was going to stay in the department. He said okay; we would continue running one side. I said okay.

One day Mr. Forehand came to me. he said that J.R. wanted me to cut my own glass. I asked him how in the world he expected me to run the line and cut my own glass. I said to Mr. Forehand, "You are the supervisor of this department, I can do one or the other. I can run the department or I can cut for the line. It doesn't matter with me; but I can't do both." I told him that I couldn't train these people and watch them, too. He looked at me as though he was shocked and said, "Don't worry about the employees; that's my job." I said, "Sure, no problem." I begin cutting glass, and then the department was heading back into a mess. Then Mr. Minich knew he had to do something quick or the whole department was going to collapse. Mr. Forehand went to him and told him to go ahead and give the department to George Brown. He said that George was better at running the department than he was.

He came to me and said, "George, you said that you wanted to be the supervisor over this department. Well, you got it." I asked him how much would the job pay. He told me ten dollars an hour and one and a half percent of everything shipped if I could handle the job. I told him handling the job isn't a problem, but why would I want to take on all that responsibility for ten dollars an hour when I made more than that now? I told him that I would accept the job for twelve dollars an hour plus bonus. He said, "I don't think that Mr. Harner will agree to that, but go ahead and I'll let you know Monday." I asked him who was going to cut the glass. He said Mr. Hendrix and Mr. Sapp. I said, "Okay, just let me know Monday," and he said okay. All of this happened on Friday.

Monday morning Mr. Minich told me, "George, you got it," and I told him thank you. I pretty much knew that I would get the job, because at the time the supervisors who were in charge were costing the company thousands of dollars every week. If he had paid me thirty dollars an hour, it still would have been in the best interests of the company, because Mr. Forehand and Mr. Morris had already cost the company enough money to pay me for three years from their mishaps.

After I was in full charge of the department, there were some questions that I had. I asked Mr. Minich if all P-175 series get 7/8 grids and 6350 series get 5/8 grids. He told me, "George, to be honest, I really don't know. You need to ask Clint. He knows more about it then I do." I asked Clint, and he said yes, that was correct. A couple weeks later, an order came in on the P-175. I asked Mr. Clint Forehand (the former supervisor) and Mr. James Jackson, the supervisor who was in charge of cutting all the grids. At that time, I didn't have a cutting section on the grid bars. They were all cut in the grid-cutting department and they both agreed.

Mr. Jackson then cut 7/8, and the line ran them. I came to find out they were supposed to have been 5/8. They tried to blame me for it. I told Mr. J.R. Minich that he was the one who told me to get the information from Mr. Forehand. I asked Mr. Jackson so that I could have a second witness. All of that was done away with because everybody was in the learning stage of the new product. But each and every one of those panels were used. The only thing we lost was time, because those windows and glass applied to their orders. I said, "Next time I have a question about something, I will get a signature." As far as I was concerned, nothing like that was going to happen again under my watch, and I was sure of that. From that point on, I checked and double checked for errors on the orders, because regardless who made the mistakes, Mr. Harner and Mr. Minich would try to blame me if it was in my department.

They tried to blame me for punches being off when the engineer himself had the punches off. Mr. Steve Landsman brought out the new punch chart for the picture windows. There are a lot of picture windows in the market with off-punched grids, because the engineer made an over sight. The grids were not crooked, they just wouldn't match up to any windows with grids. I suppose they soon forgot who it was that straightened that department out. Mr. J.R. Minich called his cousin to come down, but at the time I didn't know that Mr. Brad was his cousin. Mr. Harner and Mr. Minich made him supervisor over all of the glass houses. I didn't understand that either, because I had to teach him a lot about the glass production and the procedures of the operation. I didn't mind that, because

I tried to get the tools that I needed to make the operation of production more successful by reducing overtime.

I needed full-time employees. They wouldn't hire them for me. I needed a saw, and they wouldn't give it to me. I needed a 5/8 grid puncher, and they wouldn't give that to me. The assembly employees had to go all the way up front in order to get repairs for any 5/8 grids. I needed glass set up in the department, and they wouldn't do that either. I needed a glasscutter to cut glass, and they wouldn't give me one. Every glass house had a glasscutter except the one that I was over; I don't call that teamwork.

If you deny everything that a person needs to operate, how does one perform? Well, with me it was with God and preplanning. It was a difficult task; but I accomplished it. They didn't like it, but due to the success it was bringing the company, they accepted it. It was drawing in contracts because the customers loved the windows and they didn't have any choice but to go along with it. That's why Mr. Minich brought his cousin in to take the credit. I didn't mind that as long as I could get what I needed. I could get it through Mr. Minich's cousin.

All the production was up and in full production. I was meeting the production goal up to the point where I was above the production goal. When the production of P-175 product dropped, we pitched in to help Mr. Joseph Scroggins (which is the supervisor over the 255/165 glass house), because he was unable to carry the load. He had helped me until I told Mr. Brad that I'd rather do my own glass. I had to redo it because of Mr. Scroggins screwing it up. He was causing me to work harder in order to fix what he messed up.

They really didn't understand how I succeeded when they tried everything they could to make me fail. It was all due to wisdom and experience. It's hard to block a good man who knows what he is doing.

These are some of the tools I used to help me accomplish the success I had at MI Home Product Inc. I did them on my computer at home in order to watch my back when I wasn't there on the line to help me keep the employees straightened out and on task without me being there every time something went wrong.

P-175 Rules And Regulations

(1) HORSE PLAY OR DISORDERLY CONDUCT
(2) LEAVING ASSIGNED WORK AREA OR COMPAN
     PREMISES WITHOUT AUTHORIZATION
(3) INTERFERING WITH THE WORK OF OTHER
     EMPLOYEES
(4) USE OF ABUSIVE OR PROFANE LANGUAGE
     TOWARD ANOTHER EMPLOYEE
(5) MUST WEAR SAFETY EQUIPMENTS
(6) REPORTING TO LINE LATE AFTER CLOCK IN
(7) UNABLE TO FULLFILL JOB ASSIGNMENT
(8) EXCESSIVE USE OF BATHROOM
(9) POOR QUALITY IN PRODUCTION FINISH
     PRODUCT
(10) KEEPING CLEAN WORKING AREA
(11) REFUSAL TO PERFORM JOB ASSIGNMENT GIVI
     BY SUPERVISOR
(12) LEAVING TRASH IN WORK AREA

Please read these rules and regulations because it can affect
your job. An employee that focus on what they're doing
perform good quality in their finish product.

George Brown
P-175 supervisor
Glass House #3

This was a reminder to the employees of the rules and conduct regulations
of what they can and could not do. It was given to each and every employee in
my department to help them understand how important it was to their job. I also
posted one on the washer guard for a daily reminder.

P-175 & 6350 SERIES OF THICKNESS SETTING
SSB GLASS = ½ SWIGGLE, DSB AND TEMPER
GLASS 7/16 SWIGGLE @ 687

450 SERIES OF THICKNESS SETTING
SSB =7/16 SWIGGLE, DSB AND TEMPER GLASS
@ 3/8 SWIGGLE @ 625

155,255, 355, AND 165, 178 SERIES OF
THICKNESS SETTING, SSB = 5/16 , DSB AND
TEMPER GLASS =1/4 @ 500 WITH AIR INSIDE
PANEL.
NO TOUCH UP, ALL TOUCH UP WILL BE
DONE AT GRID TABLE, GRIDS INSTALLERS
KEEP TOUCH UP PAINT AWAY FROM GRIDS.
MAKE SURE YOU'RE USING THE RIGHT
PATTERN WHEN INSTALL 2,3, & 4 LITES.

BY: GEORGE BROWN

They wouldn't give me any old employees to help train the new employees
so I had to use these graphics in order for them to have a guide in order to meet

production without any help; all the Swiggle windows glass houses had a lead person except for me.

$13 \frac{21}{32}$ $28\frac{3}{4}$ $43\frac{1}{2}$ — ⌒ ⌐ ⌣

$10 \frac{21}{32}$ $22\frac{3}{4}$ $34\frac{1}{2}$ — 40

$7\frac{21}{32}$ $16\frac{3}{4}$ $25\frac{1}{2}$ — 30

$11\frac{1}{8}$ $22\frac{3}{16}$ $34\frac{3}{4}$ $46\frac{31}{32}$ $58\frac{1}{32}$ — 60^{EQ}

$13\frac{21}{32}$ — $28\frac{3}{4}$ — $42\frac{31}{32}$ — $56\frac{1}{32}$ — 60^{OR}

—— $175\,P$ ——

This graphic was pass out to replace the old graphic that had the wrong figurations and many units was shipped out wrong. It were given to me to pass out to the employees. I was told to throw away the old punch sheets that the grid ladies been punching because they were wrong initially. Nobody was blamed for that incident. How is it that I can't make one mistake, and they make many mistakes and nothing is done about it? What is the problem? Because of that, I made sure that I didn't make any mistakes on my part. They fought so hard against me ever since I came back to MI Home Inc. before and after a false lay off. I remade the picture window cut sheet in order for the employees to better understand what it was that they were reading. This is a copy of the picture window cutting sheet that I passed out to the employees. I didn't understand why they refused to give me any experienced employees to help train the new employees. I had to constantly leave the line to go all the way to another department up front to get parts for my line to work with.

P-175 PICTURE WINDOWS

30 H	7 21/32	16 ¾	25 ½		
40 H	10 21/32	22 ¾	34 ½		
50 H	13 21/32	28 ¾	43 ½		
60 H	11 1/8	22 3/16	34 ¾	46 21/32	58 ½ EQ
60 H OR	13 21/32	28 ¾	42 31/32	56 ½	

THE FIRST PUNCH IS ALWAYS AT THE TOP OF ALL P-175 PICTURE WINDOWS, UNLESS SPECIAL PUNCHES IS REQUESTED BY THE CUSTOMER

BY: GEORGE BROWN

The main reason for me putting so much into this line so the employees can clearly see what they was reading.I wanted everything to be perfectly clear to everyone on my team. After I'd gotten the department into a productive line, I had former employees who wanted to be transferred to my line when in the beginning they were running away from it. Nobody knew what to do or what they were doing. Before I took over, they wanted to punish the employees for doing what their supervisor told them to do. I thought that they were wrong. They wanted to blame me for something that I didn't tell them to do, because it's my department.

As things continued on, Mr. Ronnie Stucky started drinking more and more on the job. He started cursing his employees out for something that they didn't do because he was too drunk to think normally. He was confused about where he stood on his production and took it out on his employees. If I could smell the alcohol, so could Mr. Lynn Harner and Mr. J.R. Minich, as close as he was to them. I had to help him out many times. Ms. Wanda Lewis witnessed it many times.

At one time I ran some picture windows, and Mr. Stucky told Mr. J.R. Minich that I didn't run them. I told him that I did, because Mr. Stucky had rebuilt some more frames. Mr. Minich sided with him. I said to him, "If I didn't run that glass, there where is it?" Mr. Minich told both of us to come with him. He went and pulled the temper glass order sheet and saw where the glass had come in. We then went back to Mr. Stucky's department and looked at the order, but the order numbers were different. He had put the wrong tickets on the order. The tickets that he used weren't even scheduled for that week but the next week. The glass hadn't made it in for the second order, and shipping had loaded it on the truck. The order had the wrong numbers on it, and nothing was done about it. Yet they were ready to blame me for something that two other supervisors had done.

We had run some argon gas panels and a new employee forgot to put gas in it. The order had it written on there, but she forgot. Mr. Stucky held a grudge on me. He tried to blame me for running the panels. I told him that the glass wasn't ready. I was walking by at lunch time and saw that Ms. Cindy Lariscy had started taping that glass. I took it off the table and put it back on the buggy. Then I pushed it back into a hole. Before I could get back there after lunch due to hunting for tempered glass up front, someone got it back and started running it. Mr. Steve Landsman called me on the radio and told me to come back there immediately. I thought someone had gotten hurt on the line, so I stopped pulling the tempered glass and rushed back there. Mr. Stucky had told Mr. Landsman that I told him to run that glass. I told Mr. Landsman that was a lie. I said, "If I told him to run it, then why when I passed by there at lunch time I took it off the table and put it back on the buggy and pushed it back into a hole?" Mr. Lynn Harner and Mr. J.R. Minich called me to the office later on that day and asked me the same question that Mr. Landsman asked. I told them the same thing.

Mr. Harner replied, "What if we ask Cindy, and she says no?" I told them to go ahead because I didn't see why she would lie, and that killed that.

About three weeks later, Mr. Brad told me to come with him. I said, "Okay, just give me a minute." When I got there, the next thing I knew he had disciplinary papers in his hand for that same incident that happened weeks prior. I told him that I wasn't going to sign it. Why would I want to sign something that I know I didn't do? Then he said, "How about this one" You did this, didn't you?" I told him, "Brad, you should be ashamed of yourself. You weren't even here when this took place. Mr. Minich had bypassed that because everybody was in the learning process, and besides we used all of those panels." I told him to give it to me and I'd sign it because I knew that I would never get another one on my part. Later I found out that they added some more wording to it. I went back and did what I do best, and that is run production.

Then orders started going down, and they decided to move the P-175 glass production over to the patio glass house and Mr. James Prescott was the supervisor over the patio glass. I was over the P-175 series part. Mr. Prescott thought that I was sent over there to take over. He was intimidated by me being over there; it caused a conflict. I gave it all to Mr. Prescott and went back to cutting glass. Mr. J.R. Minich came over to the Optimizer looking for me. He asked Mr. Hendrix where I was, and Mr. Hendrix told him that I was in the back pulling glass. Mr. Minich came down there and said to me, "You wanted to be supervisor, you got it." I asked him about Mr. Prescott. He told me not to worry about him. He said that he had told Mr. Prescott that he would be working under me. I told him okay.

I turned that patio glass house around. There was a big difference in the production during the time that I was running it than when the other supervisor ran it. During my time of running production in that department, it surpassed the production that he was running. That was because of Mr. James Prescott being disorganized. After I took the patio glass department, it was back in business. They didn't have to wait for any panels, and they didn't have any back orders. As we continued to run production, the orders really picked up for the P-175 glass house. They also started back up the P-175 glass in its own department. They continued running it in the patio glass house also.

Mr. Brad had Mr. J.R. Minich hire some more employees in order to run production. Mr. Brad tried to train them how to run the operation of production in the P-175 glass house, and they were making a mess. I had to run back and forth because Mr. Brad didn't know what he was doing. Then Mr. J.R. Minich told me to go back to the P-175 glass house, and he would put Mr. Clint Forehand over the patio glass house.

Every time you turned around Mr. Ronnie Stucky kept talking about running out of glass. He was breaking it like a crazy man because the worker over there didn't understand how to install the insulated glass panels. They took their plastic hammers and beat the beads into the glass. They weren't supposed to beat them in, but tap them in, and that makes a big difference. When you beat the bead in between the glass and the frame, it will break most of the time. That results into high cost for glass breakage, which was due to improperly installing glass in the windows frames.

They were breaking so much glass over there until he started lying about not getting the right count on his panels. I found out that he was charging some of his broken glass to my department. He was saying they were broken on the cart. He really had Mr. Harner believing Mr. Stucky, even after catching him lying many times before. I asked Mr. Harner where was the glass that was broken on the cart. He showed me the cart that was supposed to have broken glass on it. I asked him if that glass was broken on the cart, then why did it have tape on it and a window sticker? They only put window stickers on them when they are in the frame. He couldn't answer that question because he knew that Mr. Stucky was lying before he even came over to me and asked me about the broken glass.

The problem was before I took charge, Mr. Ronnie Stucky had a reason for not meeting his production. But after I took charge over the P-175 glass house, he no longer had that excuse. I came up with a solution to end that situation by having a check-off list that I made up at home. I showed it to Mr. Brad, and he showed it to Mr. J.R. Minich. They approved it. I was to go ahead and use it. It became a great tool to keep the leaders honest about receiving their materials in order to complete their product. He soon had to find another excuse for not meeting his production schedule on time and not blame it on glass, because that option was no longer available for him to use.

 # GLASS VERIFICATION

P-175 GLASS HOUSE #3
SUPERVISOR: GEORGE BROWN

LETTER _____

SIZE_____   AMOUNT_____

SIZE_____   AMOUNT_____

SIZE_____   AMOUNT_____

SIZE_____   AMOUNT_____

SIZE_____   AMOUNT_____

SIZE_____   AMOUNT_____

SIZE_____   AMOUNT_____

SIZE_____   AMOUNT_____

SIZE_____   AMOUNT_____

SIZE_____   AMOUNT_____

_____
SIGNATURE

In order to get a buggy of glass, the puller would have to sign this form and acknowledge that all the glass was on the buggy and accounted for before the glass handler could pull it. Therefore there wouldn't be any misunderstanding. There was a time when the P-175 window line was breaking so much glass, sometimes I thought that I was running the order over. Mr. Ronnie Stucky didn't know where he was most of the time in production. He was constantly running back and forth to his car drinking and coming back into the plant cursing his employees because he didn't have a clue where he was at in his production. He was ordering glass he didn't even need. We would run the repairs, and he'd finish running his windows. There still would be repairs that he ordered sitting on the rack.

The two people that were actually running

Mr. Stucky line were (Mr. Ronnie Allen and Mr. Dave Hunter.) Mr. Ronnie Stucky caused Mr. Ford so much trouble, until he got tired of it. He went to the human resource office and complained about his attitude and drinking problem. Mr. Lee Wilson refused to investigate the matter. Mr. Ford wasn't the only one complaining about Mr. Stucky harassing him. There were many others also. Mr. Stucky didn't take that complaint seriously when Mr. Wilson didn't do anything. He just continued on harassing his employees. Eventually, Mr. Ford left the company because he couldn't get any help through the human resource office. After Mr. Ford left, Mr. Stucky became even more aggressive and started harassing Mr. Scott.

Mr. Stucky came to me on many occasions to ask for my help about an issue he had on a window. I would always help him. After all I did for him, he still would run back and forth to Mr. Lynn Harner telling him lies. He would say that he didn't have glass for this or that, and every time Mr. Lynn Harner came to the line, he would always find the order completed. I knew that Mr. Stucky was drunk. I didn't say anything because I knew that Mr. Lynn Harner and Mr. J.R. Minich knew it, too. If I could smell the alcohol without standing close to him, I knew as close as he was to Mr. Harner and Mr.Minich, they could smell it, too. So why wasn't he terminated? I knew somewhere down the line sooner or later it would end. I was hoping that it would be sooner than later for the benefit of the company. He began to start interfering with my department. I told him not to interfere with my employees. They were already running the way I'd set them up to run. He said, "Okay, I'll just come to you when I need something." I told him that would be the best policy.

I also came up with this report. When a supervisor borrows an employee and doesn't want to own up to it and not correctly report their time to payroll, I could have something to look back on and keep track on the transfer hours and the glass breakage that was leaving from my department. I assigned Ms. Rita Greene to the finished good panel sheets. I told her not to let anyone get anything unless the sheet is signed. The P-175 window line supervisor Mr. Ronnie Stucky or his employees accounted for the glass on that buggy due to untruthfulness.

GEORGE BROWN
P-175/6350 GLASS HOUSE #3   BEGINNING DATE

_____

GLASS HOUSE #3 WEEKLY REPORT

DAYS	HOURS	UNITS RAN	UNITS PMH	GLASS SCRAP	DEPT SCRAP CHARGE TO	DESCRIPTION
MONDAY						
TUESDAY						
WEDNESDAY						
THURSDAY						
FRIDAY						
SATURDAY						
TOTAL						

DAILY CHARGE OUT HOURS TO OTHER DEPARTMENTS

DAYS	TRANFER HOURS	DEPARTMENT #	MAINTENANCE	DESCRIPTION
MONDAY				
TUESDAY				
WEDNESDAY				
THURSDAY				
FRIDAY				
SATURDAY				
TOTAL				

_____

SUPERVISOR SIGNATURE

On the next page will be a report by the quality control supervisor.

DATE	2-9-04	2-10-04	2-11-04	2-12-04	2-13-04
Total's	114	71	133	26	15
Utility	Monday	Tuesday	Wednesday	Thursday	Friday
6-350	LOADER - 1	LINE - 9			
GH 1	3 BROKE 10 BAD GRID	4	4	3	2
GH 2	9 " 33 " "	7	5	7	2
GH 3	10 "	3	5	10	0
450 Line	Monday	Tuesday	Wednesday	Thursday	Friday
	LINE - 29	LINE - 4	LINE - 6	CART - 2	LINE - 1
			CART - 1		
			CUST - 4		
P-175	Monday	Tuesday	Wednesday	Thursday	Friday
	LINE - 2	LINE - 26	LINE - 64		
		STACK - 6	CART - 1		
			TAPER - 2		
			STACK - 12		
			WRONG GLASS -24		
Spec. Line	Monday	Tuesday	Wednesday	Thursday	Friday
	BAD GRID - 1	LINE - 1	BAD GRID - 1	BAD GRID - 4	BAD GRID - 1
		BAD SQUIGGLE-5			
		WRONG SIZE - 1			
255 Line	Monday	Tuesday	Wednesday	Thursday	Friday
	LINE - 2	LINE - 1			
	CART - 2	CART - 3			
	SLIGHT LINE - 5				
165 Line	Monday	Tuesday	Wednesday	Thursday	Friday
	LINE - 3	CART - 1	LINE - 1		LINE - 7
	STACK - 1		CART - 3		CART - 2
	SCRATCHED - 1				MISSING - 23
	BOW E - 2				

This report right here is a good week for the P-175 window line, and they didn't turn in the glass report for Thursday or Friday. As you can see on this report, all the glass houses turned in their glass breakage. The window lines refused to turn theirs in because they constantly tried to hide their breakage. You will see repair tickets where it says missing, and sometimes they would try to order insulated glass panels without a ticket.

I told my employees on the P-175 glass house line not to do any repairs without the proper paperwork. Because I wouldn't be able to allow them to count it into their production due to the lack of paperwork to show what they done. Therefore they would lose money. I didn't have to remind them because they already knew where I stood when it came to paperwork. The biggest problem was having supervisors working against one another, and upper management couldn't or wouldn't stop it. So as time progressed, I was called to jury duty in the County of Emanuel. This took place February 2, 2004, by the Deputy Clerk Mr. Jay Lawson. I returned back to work on a Monday, which was February 17, 2004, after being released of duty.

EMANUEL COUNTY, GEORGIA
SUPERIOR COURT

2-2-04

THIS IS TO CERTIFY THAT George Brown WAS IN EMANUEL SUPERIOR COURT ON 2-2-04 and DATE(S). To return each day until trial complete.

DEPUTY CLERK

Clerk

I gave a copy to my employer and payroll. Mrs. Linda Wiggins was the payroll clerk. Mr. J.R. Minich placed Mr. Brad in charge of my department while I was on jury duty, which lasted for two weeks. I traveled over forty miles a day to set things up for the day production up to the last week. Mr. Brad approached me and said, "You don't think that I can run this department, do you?" I said, "No, it's not that; I just want to make sure everything is going okay." But really in my mind I knew he couldn't run it for a long period of time. The last four days I gave him full control.

When I got back to work, the whole department was in a mess. Nobody complained about the condition that the department was in or the amount of glass that was wasted. Mrs. Davis (the assistant hr) told me, "George, when you were out, your employees didn't make anything." She said that she felt sorry for them and gave them ten dollars per hour.

Mr. Brad had an order cut by the grid cutting department and assembled together by the assembling table that was supposed to have been six lites, but instead of making them six lites the grids cutting department cut them in the original lites, which would be a four lites. The line had fallen behind in production, because of lack of leadership. I told Mr. Brad to continue watching the line until I could straighten it out.

They had glass and empty carts everywhere in that department. It made it almost impossible to walk through the department without getting cut, because glass was sticking out everywhere. I met Mr. J.R. Minich coming down from the office and I asked him how in the world the department got into this mess? He replied that they had a bad week. I told Mr. Minich that Mr. Brad was going to continue running the line while I cleaned the department up. Mr. Minich said okay.

At 9:30 am we had a meeting that lasted a little more than an hour. From that meeting I went straight into another meeting with Mr. Brad, which lasted to about 12:00 pm. During this time in between those meetings that glass was run; I never got a chance to see the grids. If the order had been written up right and the grid department, the assemble table, the toppers, and anybody else had the order, then the person who was in charge when this order was started was Mr. Brad. To me, he was solely responsible for the mishap in the order, not me. I was the only one who had it right and was the only one punished for an incident that wasn't my fault. Mr. Jackson and Mr. Brad, which are both white supervisors, were the main ones involved in this incident. They were both there when it began.

On February 18, 2004, I had to feed the glass because Mr. Brad failed to tell me that Mr. Antonio Reese would be off due to a doctor appointment in Augusta. I had to work instead of supervising the line. Mr. Brad was in fact still supervising the line as of February 19, 2004. Mr. Reese had to go back for some X-rays to be taken at the hospital in Augusta. I still had to work on the line, and Mr. Brad was actually still in charge of the line even though I was back. Due to lack of help, he had to do my job and I had to do the job of an employee.

My termination was decided without even discussing the incident with me. It seems impossible to make a decision without hearing both sides—the accusing party and the defendant. I said to Mr. Lee Wilson, "What is this?" He told me that Mr. Lynn Harner told him to terminate George Brown and he had no choice. I asked for what? Mr. Wilson told me, "For two hundred and sixteen panels you ran wrong." I said to him, "I ran wrong? Lee, you know that I wasn't here for two weeks. Those panels were cut by Mr. James Jackson and fabricated under the leadership of Mr. Brad." I told him that when those panels were run, I was in a meeting. He told me to go downstairs and talk to Mr. Harner, and I said okay.

I went to Mr. Harner's office and spoke with him concerning the incident. I told him that those grids were cut and fabricated while I was on jury duty. Mr. Lynn Harner said, "It is your department, George." I said, "Yes, it is, but there's nothing I can do when I'm not here." I reminded him that when an employee fails to follow a supervisor's instruction, you write the employee up not the supervisor. The order that they had was written up correctly, but the employee failed to follow instructions. All of that was done under Mr. Brad's watch, not mine. He said the decision had been made, and it's going to stand.

Before I took that department it was all broken, no organization, no leadership, and no sense of direction. After I built that department to be successful, Mr. J.R. Minich and Mr. Lynn Harner thought that it could run on its own. They were sadly mistaken. They would finally realize that it wasn't as easy as they thought it was by just seeing how the production was flowing through that department. It took more than just a body to present there; it took the ability of someone who had true leadership and could adjust to any situation and still be able to perform. All of the good things that happened in that department weren't because of Mr. Brad, and they could see that clearly after I, Mr. George Brown, was longer there.

Mr. Brad did everything that he could possibly do in order to keep that department together, and it began to go downhill because of his inability to run the department. They removed him and sent him to another department. They did not know that he was only acting off of the information that I gave him. They thought it was coming from him, so they accepted it. Mr. Brad was removed because he was messing up too much insulated glass that had to be thrown away. After they moved him out, they tried Mr. Antonio Reese, and that didn't work. He got tired of the situation and requested a transfer and moved on to another job. Then they tried Mr. Gary Ogden, and that didn't work out. They tried Mr. Steve Landsman, and that didn't work out. They then tried to combine Mr. Landsman and Mr. Ogden together, and that didn't work out.

Ms. Wanda Lewis was the best qualified person on the line. I personally worked with her, and she didn't have anyone to go to for advice when a problem arose. She told them that if they didn't call George Brown back to that department, it would go down. All the supervisors that they put over that line messed up thousands of dollars of materials, and nothing was done. When I was no longer there and the employees realized that they weren't going to call me (George Brown) back, they started quitting and getting transferred off the line. After they saw that there wasn't anything else that they could do for that department, they shut down the Swiggle glass house for the P-175. They were not concerned about the company interests, only their own.

I was terminated from MI Home Product Inc. I waited a couple of days to see if they were going to call me back. I went to the Georgia Department of Labor for workmen compensation and applied for benefits. My separation notice listed that my termination was involuntary. The Labor Department wanted to know what the reason was for my termination. I told them that I went to jury duty for two weeks, and after I returned to work I was involuntary terminated. They told me that that wasn't right. They suggested that I talk to EEOC, and they could help me get my job back. I told him thanks for the advice and the information. This is a copy of the report that the Georgia Department of Labor Claims Examiner's Determination. They sent this to me after they heard both sides of the story, and then they made their decision based on the facts.

In section 3 this report said because I wasn't the only person responsible for the work. Therefore, I was not in control of the condition that led to my discharge. You cannot be held responsible if the work was unsatisfactory due to reasons beyond your control. They weren't there and didn't know what happened. They just heard both sides of the incident and made their decision, unlike Mr. Lynn Harner. I personally believe it was a "black and white" issue. The actual ones that are responsible are the two white supervisors, and they were the ones who should have been blamed if anyone should have.

This is a copy of the order that I was held responsible for. The order was written up correctly, therefore I don't see where I should have been blamed at all due to the fact that was presented to Mr. Lynn Harner. I sent a copy to Mr. Pete Desoto who had the final say in the matter. I didn't hear anything from him. I thought that he was a fair man—until this incident.

DOL-4428 I(R-12/03)
NM 2006

GEORGIA DEPARTMENT OF LABOR
CLAIMS EXAMINER'S DETERMINATION

BYB ___03/04/04___

CWB ___02/29/04___

SSN ~~_____~~

CAREER CENTER
5600
STATESBORO
62 PACKING HOUSE ROAD
P.O. BOX 558
STATESBORO, GEORGIA 30458
FAX # (912) 681-5228

7000

CLAIMANT	EMPLOYER
GEORGE BROWN P.O. BOX 576 TWINCITY GA 30471	J T WALKER INDUSTRIES INC DBA MI HOME PRODUCTS, INC P O BOX 1038 MILLEN GA 30442

SECTION I - CLAIM DETERMINATION

Benefits are allowed as of 02/29/04.

SECTION II - LEGAL BASIS FOR DETERMINATION

Section 34-8-194 (2) (B) (i) of the Employment Security Law says that you can be paid unemployment benefits if you were fired for failure to perform your job duties, but you made a good faith effort and were simply unable to do the work. The law says that your employer has to show that discharge or suspension was for a reason that would not allow you to be paid unemployment benefits. If you cannot be paid unemployment benefits under this section of the law, you may qualify at a later time. To do this, you must find other work and earn wages covered under unemployment law. The covered wages must be at least ten times the weekly amount of your claim. If you then become unemployed through no fault of your own, you may reapply for unemployment benefits.

SECTION III - REASONING

You were fired because of unsatisfactory work performance. You had been warned about your performance. However, the facts show you were not the only person responsible for the work. Therefore, you were not in control of the condition that lead to your discharge. You cannot be held responsible if the work was unsatisfactory due to reasons beyond your control. Therefore, you can be paid unemployment benefits.

SECTION IV - ACCOUNT CHARGEABILITY

NOTICE TO EMPLOYER:

SECTION V - APPEAL RIGHTS

NOTE: This determination will become final unless you file an appeal on or before 04/06/04. If you file an appeal you must continue to report on your claim as instructed, or you will not be paid if you win your appeal. Refer to the Claimant Handbook booklet or contact an office of the Georgia Department of Labor for more details.

Georgia Department of Labor	03/17/04	03/22/04
Claims Examiner	Date of Interview	Release Date

75

Batch Set   Z   Select Date 02\20\04   UNITS   2-18

Plant   Pull Group   Load Date   Sequence   Total
120 MILLEN   P175 PEACH 175 SH   02/20/04 to 02/20/04   65748 to 65755   0

Product Line-Color	**LABELS** **SKU-#**	Width	Height	DIM3	Width	Height	DIM3	Width/Height
		---MAIN---			***---GLASS---***			****--SCREEN---***

P175 WH   Trk-Rte:99 23 3/8   71 13/16   20 7/8   33 15/16   — 1
MARLYN DEVELOPMENT CORP   CAPITOL   19 15/16 33 15/16   1 1/7
PO#: P008304
ORD#: 1452527 .18.1 Seq 65748   Qty   1 2060EQ,SPS,WH,FIN,5/8"FLAT,6/1,INS,SSB,2
                                       CAM

P175 WH   Trk-Rte:99 23 3/8   71 13/16   20 7/8   33 15/16   — 33
MARLYN DEVELOPMENT CORP   CAPITOL   19 15/16 33 15/16   — 33÷ 5/8
PO#: P008304   Grids
ORD#: 1452527 .22.2 Seq 65749   Qty 33 TRIPLE,FAC MULL,CONT H/S,2060EQ,SPS,WH,F
                                      IN,5/8"FLAT,6/1,INS,SSB,2 CAM

Special Instructions MULL WITH SELF
                     MULL W SELF

P175 WH   Trk-Rte:99 35 3/8   59 13/16   32 7/8   27 15/16   — 280
MARLYN DEVELOPMENT CORP   CAPITOL   31 15/16 27 15/16   — 280
PO#: P008304
ORD#: 1452527 .15.2 Seq 65750   Qty 276 TWIN,FAC MULL,CONT H/S,3050,SPS,CHAR-FIB
                                      ER,WH,FIN,5/8"FLAT,6/6HORZ,INS,SSB,2 CAM

Special Instructions MULL WITH SELF
                     MULL W SELF

P175 WH   Trk-Rte:99 35 3/8   59 13/16   32 7/8   27 15/16   — 115
MARLYN DEVELOPMENT CORP   CAPITOL   31 15/16 27 15/16   — 115
PO#: P008304
ORD#: 1452527 .7.1 Seq 65751   Qty 110 3050,SPS,CHAR-FIBER,WH,FIN,5/8"FLAT,6/6H
                                      ORZ,INS,SSB,2 CAM

P175 WH   Trk-Rte:99 31 3/8   59 13/16   28 7/8   27 15/16   — — 290
MARLYN DEVELOPMENT CORP   CAPITOL   27 15/16 27 15/16   — 290
PO#: P008304
ORD#: 1452527 .5.2 Seq 65752   Qty 284 TWIN,FAC MULL,CONT H/S,2850,SPS,CHAR-FIB
                                      ER,WH,FIN,5/8"FLAT,6/6HORZ,INS,SSB,2 CAM

Special Instructions MULL WITH SELF
                     MULL W SELF

P175 WH   Trk-Rte:99 23 3/8   59 13/16   20 7/8   27 15/16   — 110
MARLYN DEVELOPMENT CORP   CAPITOL   19 15/16 27 15/16   — 110

```
HOME PRODUCTS (LIVE)                    Production Report                              Page    2
EDWORK JCR964A) (L3M)                                                         04:22PM - 12 FEB 04

Batch Set      Z                Select Date  02\20\04    UNITS
                                                                                       2-18
'lant           Pull Group               Load Date        Sequence      Total
20 MILLEN       P175  PEACH 175 SH        02/20/04 to 02/20/04  65748 to 65755    0

                        ***--------MAIN--------***  ***--------GLASS--------***  ****--SCREEN----***
'roduct Line-Color      **LABELS** Width   Height   DIM3    Width   Height   DIM3       Width/Height
                        **SKU-#**  -------- --------- --------- --------- --------- --------- ------------------
'O#: P008304
IRD#: 1452527 .9.2  Seq 65753   Qty    108 TRIPLE,FAC MULL,CONT H/S,2050,SPS,WH,FIN
                                           ,5/8"FLAT,6/6HORZ,INS,SSB,2 CAM


                     Special Instructions M U L L   W I T H   S E L F
                                          MULL W SELF

'175 WH                 Trk-Rte:99  29 3/8    47 13/16        26 7/8   21 15/16    - 16
IARLYN DEVELOPMENT CORP CAPITOL                               25 15/16 21 15/16    - 16'
'O#: P008304
IRD#: 1452527 .24.1 Seq 65754   Qty    16 2640,SPS,WH,FIN,5/8"FLAT,6/1,INS,SSB,2 C
                                          AM

175 WH                  Trk-Rte:99  23 3/8    47 13/16        20 7/8   21 15/16    - 3
ARLYN DEVELOPMENT CORP  CAPITOL                               19 15/16 21 15/16  v - 3'
RD#: P008304
RD#: 1452527 .20.2 Seq 65755   Qty     3 TRIPLE,FAC MULL,CONT H/S,2040,SPS,WH,FIN
                                          ,5/8"FLAT,6/1,INS,SSB,2 CAM


                     Special Instructions M U L L   W I T H   S E L F
                                          MULL SELF

otal For P175                831
```

On this page, look at the P.O. number p008304 and order number 1452527 shipped to Marlyn Development Corporation. You will find this order never had been changed by me. It was sent out like this from the scheduling department, and nothing on it was changed except for me putting in the amount of panels for the department to produce. It said 6/6 when they handed it out to me, and it also said 6/6 when it went into production. It was also given to Mr. James Jackson as 6/6, and he cut it 4/4. Mr. Brad allowed the grid assembling employees to fabricate it 4/4.

I wrote Mr. Mike Jackson, President of MI Home Product Inc., and later found out that he was no longer with the company. I then wrote a letter to Mr. Pete Desoto explaining to him what had happened. I waited, and I never heard from him. I then took the advice of the worker at the Georgia Department of Labor and went to EEOC in order to receive my job back. I filled out a complaint and sat down and explained to Mrs. Rudolph about what had taken place on my job at MI Home Product Inc. She told me the only conclusion that she could come to was that Mr. James Jackson, who cut the work, and Mr. Brad, who was in charge of the work during my absence, were white, and I was the only black person involved. I was the only one terminated for the incident. This had taken place on March 29, 2004. She asked me if I had any witnesses. I told her that I had witnesses that could tell her that I wasn't there when the incident was cut and fabricated. They could testify that it was done by Mr. James Jackson and Mr. Brad who were my white co-workers. When that glass was run, I was in a meeting, and after that I had to fill in to help keep production going. There was an employee out due to an illness, and because of that Mr. Brad was still running that line. Mr. Minich knew that.

These were a few mishaps that Mr. James Jackson did. He was my white co-worker in addition to working on the last project that I was terminated for and had no part in. Mr. Jackson cut eight hundred grid bar frames wrong, the same ones that I was later written up for. The person who signed the form wasn't even with the plant in Millen when this happened. He cut four hundred grid bars that had to be thrown away, and then he cut five hundred more grid bars that had to be thrown away. Mr. Jackson had an order to go by, and the grids weren't cut according to what was on the order. He cut and punched eighty grid bar frames of 40/40 picture windows, sixteen lite. We had to throw them away due to wrong punches.

The biggest incident was when he cut over a thousand grid bar frames for the 165 series, and they were being assembled by two departments. I went over to check the grids. They had a big split in them. I called the quality control supervisor Mr. Steve Landsman and discussed it with him as I thought they weren't any good. The other department had built hundreds of grid bar frames. We had to tear them down and save what endpins we could in the order to save something. There wasn't anything done to Mr. Jackson by the human resource manager or anybody else.

These are some of the witnesses that I had. I sent their statements to Ms. Janice D. Smith. She never contacted any of them in any shape or form. She had their address and phone numbers. Every time I called her, she would tell me that she was still investigating it. She later began to say that she was waiting for them to reply back to her. The witnesses that I sent her are as follows: Mrs. Brenda Percell, Mr. Richard Sapp, Mr. David Reese, Mr. Charlie Pierce, and Ms. Ann English, and many others whom names I won't include due to them still being employed with the company. I don't want any hardship to fall upon them for speaking the truth against their employer. They have an idea what will happen to them if they speak out. They have seen firsthand of how MI Home Product Inc. treated me, George Brown, who helped them achieve recognition from the world of buyers and vendors.

I'm going to include one statement that an employee wrote. I gave a copy to Mrs. Janice D, Smith. She was an eyewitness to the incident and knew that I wasn't there when those grids were cut or made. Mr. Lynn Harner terminated me because of his hatred of me making the P-175 glass house into something that the two white supervisors couldn't. They could not find a solution to the problem themselves, but after I solved the problem they decided to terminate me when I was still on jury duty. It only became a reality when I returned back to work. They did not realize that the training wasn't completely finished. The man who was in charge during my absence didn't have the ability to run it. The department still needed a leader to keep it running properly. I often wonder how people can call themselves leaders when they can't even make easy calls when the time arises. I don't understand how one could keep such a person in charge to run the company with poor decision making.

I Brenda Percell worked up under the supervision of George Brown in 2000 and I think that the department that he supervised, was done a cordially to what the plant manager wanted because they was always giving him compliments on a job well done. When we came in our orders be already laid out for us, we knew when we were going home and what time we was coming in. I can't ever remember running out of any materials that we had to work with and I also worked under other supervisors and you ask them something and they couldn't give you a straight answer. I also worked under the supervision of George Brown in 2004 during his termination, but I couldn't understand why because the order that they claiming he's responsible for, he wasn't at the plant when we built that order, George had left and went to Jury Duty for two weeks , during this time, Brad was running the department, the work orders were not coming out on time we were having to stand around and wait for work, things were not organized, or running smoothly as it were , when George was there. Brad gave us that order and we built those grids the way they were cut from the grids department. We had done completed this order when George had returned back to work. besides every body had already knew that they could be written up from the memo that George had passed out. Most every body at Mi can tell you how George ran his department and how they had him to go to other departments and help them do their work in order to meet their load dates. Over all I think George knew the job better than any Supervisor in that plant. There were some employees quilt and some transfer to the other plant due to being unorganized and not being able to make any money after George was no longer there to keep things organize for that department to operate properly.

(478) 763-4844
Brenda Percell

Brenda Percell

10-02-04

This statement was very important to my case, and this person was never contacted. I believe that Ms. Janice D. Smith just turned her head to the truth because she was for my case or she was forced to stop investigating the case by her superior. She had more than enough evidence to prove that Mr. Lee Wilson was not telling the truth. This is what Ms. Janice D. Smith had to say concerning my charge toward MI Home Product Inc. in Millen, Georgia, which doesn't make any sense at all.

U.S. EQUAL EMPLOYMENT OPPORTUNITY COMMISSION
Savannah Local Office

410 Mall Boulevard, Suite G
Savannah, GA 31406-4821
(912) 652-4234
TTY (912) 652-4439
FAX (912) 652-4248

Charge No: 115-2004-00238
Charging Party: George Brown
Respondent: MI Home Product
Incorporated

Mr. George Brown
Post Office Box 576
Twin City, Georgia 30471

Dear Mr. Brown:

This letter will serve as our explanation concerning our determination of the merits concerning the above referenced charge of discrimination. The determination relies on the following information:

On March 29, 2004, you filed a charge with the EEOC alleging that because of your race, Black, you were disciplined and discharged from your position of Glass House Supervisor in violation fo Title VII of the Civil Rights Act of 1964, as amended.

Analysis of the evidence disclosed Respondent articulated nondiscriminatory reasons for the actions. Evidence shows Respondent employees consists of 68 Whites, 134 Blacks and 18 Hispanics. Evidence shows in 1995 you were promoted to the Glass House Supervisor and in July 2000 you were demoted to Machine Operator. In March 2003 you were laid off and recalled in June 2003 as a Machine Operator. In August 2003 you were promoted to Glass House Supervisor Lead Production position. Evidence shows Respondent was aware of your race when it promoted you twice and when you were laid off and recalled. Evidence shows that you were previously issued a "final warning" around October 10, 2003, regarding performance which stated "Future quality or performance issues could be reason for separation from the company." Evidence shows you were terminated for poor performance. Evidence shows that Respondent has disciplined Whites and have discharged them for performance issues. Evidence shows that your race had nothing to do with you termination. The evidence does not lead to the conclusion that the action(s) taken was based on your race or that the employer had discriminatory motive in the action(s).

Page 2
115-2004-00238

Enclosed please find your Dismissal and Notice of Rights and Information Sheet. If you want
to pursue your charge further, you have the right to sue the Respondent(s) named in your
charge in U.S. District Court within 90 days from the date you received the enclosed notice.
Please read the documents carefully.

Sincerely,

02-15-05
Date

Janice D. Smith
Investigator

Enclosure

    This is Ms. Janice D. Smith's conclusion. My situation wasn't based on how many different races were employed at MI Home Product Inc. My situation concerned what happened to me, which can be easily concluded to being a race issue, because of the people involved in the incident that took place. She said that the evidence showed in 1995 I was promoted to glass house supervisor and in July 2000 demoted to a machine operator. The evidence did not show the reason for me being demoted to machine operator, because there wasn't one.

Ms. Smith is an attorney. Ms. Smith saw all the loopholes Mi Home Products had in their evidence that they provided to her. Even after she herself told me I had a case due to the facts that three people were involve in this incident and two was white and one were black and only the black one were fired. She stated that I was laid off in 2003 and recalled in June 2003, but what the evidence doesn't show is the reason for me being laid off. I was more qualified than anybody in the department including the supervisor, because I'm the one who trained him in certain areas. They compared me to the other employees in the department, which was unreal. I had a better performance record, attendance, and ability to adapt to any situation when it came to production. I had the longest length of service with the company, and the evidence doesn't show why I was called back or how many employees they called back or how many employees were newly hired before I was called back. I can assure you that it wasn't because they wanted to call me back, but because Mr. Mike Jackson made them call me back.

She stated that I was promoted in August 2003 to glass house supervisor, but she doesn't show the reason why I was promoted to the P-175 glass house supervisor. I was promoted because they only had two choices. The choices were to either succeed or fail. The two white supervisors they had running it were failing and wasting materials and constantly causing the company to lose money. Therefore, they didn't have any choice but to promote me because they knew that I was the only one in the plant that could straighten that department out. After I was terminated, they had to shut down that department since they didn't have anyone who could run it. They had several others who failed. They finally had to move it out and try something else.

She stated that they had given me a final warning, but the evidence did not show any other warning that was given to me. I went ahead and signed this in order to stop being harassed, but this document had more writing added to it. When I signed this statement it had one date on it, the statement had eight hundred panels listed at the bottom, and the top part was supposed to have been scratched out. The manager who signed this statement wasn't even with the company in Millen when this happened.

MI Home Products, Inc.
Millen, GA
Final Warning Agreement

Date: 10-13-03

Employee: George Brown

SS #: ~ ~~~~~~~~~ BB

Quality Infraction _____

Product Code _____

Date of Incident 10-9-03, 10-10-03

Description of Incident:

~~See attachments~~

In Supervisory positions efficient performance of production is expected for continued employment. Future quality or performance issues could be reason for separation from the company

~~Prior Notable Incidents:~~

Manufactured 800 panels of glass with wrong grid size

The above incident demonstrates a willful disregard to perform duties in the manner expected by MI Home Products, Inc., along with disregard expected for quality products produced by MI Home Products, Inc.

This agreement is a final warning. MI Home Products, Inc., in its sole and exclusive discretion, may make the determination to follow through with a discharge if any of the following infractions are committed in the future:

    (1) Failure to meet the basic quality standards established by MI Home Products, Inc. on any job performed.
    (2) A demonstration of disregard for customer satisfaction.
    (3) A demonstration of disregard for the image of MI Home Products, Inc. to its customer.
    (4) Commits any other infraction constituting sufficient cause for immediate termination of employment.

George Brown
Employee

Ce Crofton, HR
Supervisor

Bill
Management

Why would a manager write up an incident that happened in the past? As you can see where they scratched out notes in two places, one says "see

She stated the evidence shows MI had disciplined whites and discharged them for performance issues, but it did not show that Mr. Annon Forehand was supervisor over the 450 window line and failed because of poor performance issues. He made many mistakes on that line and was broken down to a lead person. He later was promoted to supervisor over the 6350 series line. He made many mistakes and poor had performance, but it didn't cost him his job. They told him to redo the windows that he'd messed up; he refused and walked out. This is what caused him to lose his job. He came back the next day and was fired. He was surprised because this wasn't the first time he walked out and kept his job. He was the one who made the mistake.

What happened to me was caused by two white co-workers. The only part I had to do with it was that it was my department. If I'm on jury duty and not there when the incident started, who should be held accountable for that? If the employees do something wrong, then why would the supervisor be held accountable for something they did wrong on their own and not with the consent of the supervisor who is in charge of the glass house department? Then when will the employees be held accountable for something that they do wrong? You will never find a company anywhere that punishes supervisors for something they didn't tell the employees to do other than MI Home Product Inc., because that's actually what happened to me on February 19, 2004, by Mr. Lynn Harner, the general manager, and Mr. J.R. Minich, the assistant manager.

Why would a manager write up an incident that happened in the past? As you can see where they scratched out notes in two places, one says "see attachment." Then where is it? The other one says under "prior notable incidents"—there weren't any. This is the only incident that I was involved in, along with Mr. J.R. Minich (assistant plant manager). Mr. Clint Forehand, Mr. James Jackson, and Mr. Ronnie Stucky—weren't any of these people written up for this incident? Why not? The manager who signed this form wasn't even with MI Home Product Inc., which is located in Millen, Georgia, when this incident took place. Why would the human resource manager allow this form to even be written up in the first place when it was something that happened in the past? I'll tell you why—because he didn't want to call me back, so they tried everything that they could to make me fail and couldn't.

If I Mr. Brown had poor performance, then what would it be called for the first two supervisors who ran the department, who had it all out of order and bad production before I took it over? They had thousands of bad windows out in the field that I had to redo. This is what my real production chart looked like, because I always believed in doing my best in whatever I did. I was promoted in August 2003 and was above my goal of production in the new operation, along with quality. Even when I was training the newly hired employees, I was still maintaining my production through all the hardship I faced from the upper management. They were always trying to hinder me from achieving the production goals.

	Dept	$ Win Units week1	Bonus week 1	Win Units week2	$ Bonus week 2	Actual UPMH week 1	Actual UPMH week 2	UPMH Goal	Actual Scrap % week 1	Actual Scrap % week 2	Scrap % Goal	$ UPMH Bonus	$ Scrap Bonus	Total Bonus
Brown, George	GH 3	17345	179.46	14848	148.48	9.66	8.65	8	6.41	4.16	5	81.985	37.12	$447.05

The date on this sheet was November 22, 2003. Mr. J.R. Minich scratched that date out. My production and performance weren't the real problem. The real problem was that they loved what was happening, but they didn't like the one who was making it happen. That was me, George Brown. After all the written proof that I gave Ms. Janice D. Smith concerning my production with MI, she still failed to get my job back.

I would like to ask this question, where are the laws that keep things balanced between the employers and the employees? How many more families will have to suffer because the law fails to do the right thing? I often wonder how do people sleep well at night when they know they have caused great hardship to fall upon a family without any reason on the victim's part, just because they were trying to protect the company's interests or their own personal agenda? Why make rules and regulations if the company itself will not abide by them?

Before I went back there, they couldn't even get a production chart like this because they didn't have anyone with the skill to do so. Mr. James Jackson knows that I can take any production line and make it produce. He told me himself that it will pay for MI to let me go and set up all the lines. Mr. Jackson has witnessed what I have done.

They might not admit it, but MI suffered a loss when I was wrongfully terminated from the company. They are still suffering because they don't have any leaders. Oh yes they have people with leadership titles, but that doesn't make them a leader. A true leader can tell the difference between helping the company and when he or she is hurting it. I must say even though I went through some hardship, I knew who caused mine. But there are many customers who are being hit from the blind side on the purchases of windows and doors such as Granger, Fla, Robert Bowers, Premier, Wickes, Lowe's, Williams Brothers, Stock Cummings, Dave Carter and Associates, Carolina Builders, Bogart, Lake City Industries, Builders First Source, Davis Insulation, All Star, Stringer Lumber, St. Andrews, Merrifield Village, Burlington, Ocala, Elkhart, Sacred Heart Village. All of these customers could face hardships due to lawsuits or costly repairs from no fault of their own due to buying defective doors and windows with weaker glass and metal.

The doors with the inserts in the metal were thinned out. The inserts were second to third grade door inserts in order to reduce costs, because they tried raising the price of the products and it caused a reduction in sales. They then lowered the price of the product back down to solve their cost problem by the possibility of causing harm to someone else. They don't care as long as they are not held liable for the damage that their products caused. In areas especially where there are strong winds and tornados that hit at all times, there could be problems.

If you have the products that you brought from MI Home Product, check them out. You will find that every word that I have said is true and factual. I will say to any employee who may be facing a similar situation, my advice to you is to log down each and every event that happened with the date, time, and names. You should keep all the documents that you possibly can and if possible get a voice recorder and record some of the conversations that are being said between you and your employer. You should keep it in your own file for your protection. I found out that it will take that and even more, because if you don't, trying to get your job back through EEOC is a waste of your time.

This country tells us we have justice for all, but I say it's justice for some. I have found out that the laws apply to people who have money to buy their way through the system, give a little here and there in order to fix things on their behalf. They don't worry about the outcome because they know that you don't have money to counter their attacks, so they get away with it. Someone needs to step up and stand up for the right. I once heard a man say that if a man isn't willing to die for something, then he or she isn't fit to live for anything. You must not be afraid to confront your enemy, because fear will cause you to continue to accept the pressure of hardship, harassment, and mental abuse from your employer. If you are not careful, that will result in a breakdown.

These are some of the things I poured out of myself into MI for it to be successful in today's competition in the window industry world. I poured my time, loyalty, and commitment to improve production, organization, and placing employees in the right positions to fit their ability to be able to perform their job. I did all of this in order for it to be in the best interests of the company's progress in becoming the number one window company in the world.

My accomplishments at MI Home Product Inc. are as follows:

(1) From 1995 to March 2004, I took on the task of turning the patio glass department around from four to five hundred panels a day to over a thousand panels a day. This resulted in not hiring a whole second shift for the patio glass house and that saved hundreds of thousands of dollars.

(2) I was given control of ordering my own supplies and materials for my department by Mr. Steve Brush and Mr. Doug Beissel in order to avoid from having back orders. I achieved that. As time passed due to the other glass houses running out of material, Mr. Steve Brush wanted me to start ordering enough materials for all the 450, 7500, 255, 165, and the patio glass house in order to keep from having back orders.

(3) I had to help Mr. Joseph Scroggins and Mr. Alphonzo Sapp make their production in order to keep them from having back orders, which saved the company thousands of dollars.

(4) I helped achieve the Carolina Builders Vendor award of the year.

(5) I was responsible for the company receiving full control of supplying Dave Carter and Associates with all their mobile home doors and parts needs.

(6) I took on the task of the concord grids, a job that I never did before. The 450 series glass house had done some standard windows with the concord grid series, but had never done any specials. They had about two hundred specials and wanted me to do them. I asked Mr. Reed why not let Mr. Scroggins do them since he'd already done them before, and he told me, "No, I want you to do them, besides I thought you liked a challenge." I told him, "Yes, but I've never done these before." He said to me, "Well, you are going to do them." I asked him what was the formula for the concord grids, and he said he didn't have one. Then I asked him how was I supposed to put them together then? He said, "Just do it, George." The order was for about two hundred grid bar frames that had to be put together like a puzzle and each set was in twos, fours, and tens. I had to figure the sizes out myself, and Ms. Wanda Lewis cut them. It had to be done in two days and I achieved it.

(7) They brought in the intercept machine and were trying to run four different cords on it and couldn't meet production. They blamed Mr. Scroggins for not making production. I went to Mr. Steve Brush and Mr. Todd Reed and told them that it wasn't Mr. Scroggins's fault that he couldn't make production. The problem was that he was trying to make too many cord changes, which took up one-third of his time. I told them that if they hired a night shift, then that would solve the problem. They said cord changes don't have anything to do with production. They then brought in Mr. Brain Sitlinger and nothing changed. They then decided to make two shifts, and each shift ran two cords each. Production shot up.

(8) Mr. Reed purchased a True Seal Insulating Machine from True Seal Manufacturing. The company sent Mr. Alphonzo Sapp and Mrs. Tormeka Scarborough to school in order to learn how to

operate the new machine. They put me over there when it was time to run it. I didn't have any knowledge of it, and neither did they. I asked for the manual to the True Seal Machine and learned from it. I achieved it.

(9) I achieved the number one unit per man-hour in the True Seal magazine, which now reads, "MI Home Product Inc. is the number one unit per man-hour producer."

(10) They wanted to start up the Optimizer and send Mr. Charlie Brown and Mr. Joseph Scroggins to the Optimizer GED seminar class to learn how to operate it. When they returned, they didn't know much and said that the instructor had told them that because of the age of the Optimizer, it wouldn't cut but one size glass at a time when you program it manually. They wanted me to run it, and again I didn't have any training at all for the new operation. I asked Mr. Kelly if I could take the manual home and study it. He said sure. When I start working with it and messing with the programs, I found out that it would cut whatever I wanted it to cut, and I achieved it.

(11) I went to the P-175 glass house department to be a glass topper. They had two white supervisors in that department running it. They still couldn't get production going. They threw thousands of dollars away by running the glass wrong.

Mr. J.R. Minich and Mr. Lynn Harner decided to give me a try in August, and I had that department up into production in about thirty days. We were only running one side of the table until work picked up, and then we had to run both sides. When the work went back down due to the customers reorganizing their warehouse, I had to go over to the patio glass house and straighten it out. I asked myself why a company would want to fire a man for something that someone else did after all the things he'd done for the company. These are the things they did for me:

(1) Mr. Brush sent me to management seminar in Pennsylvania at MI Printing Co. in Millersburg, Pennsylvania in 1998 and 1999.

(2) Mr. Brush gave me a promotion.

(3) Then Mr. Reed started harassing me, wanting me to do something that the maintenance people couldn't do themselves.

(4) He got on his knees looking all underneath the washer trying to find something to blame me for.

(5) He falsely blamed me for something I didn't do and found out later it wasn't true.

(6) He blamed me for the machine breaking glass and couldn't tell me how many it supposed to break a day. Even the representatives couldn't tell me how many it was supposes to break a day. They always would say it depends on the temperature.

(7) Then Mr. Reed started harassing me through Ms. Robinson, Mr. Scroggins, Mr. Sapp, and Mr. Jacob, and then finally Mr. Lee Wilson with a lay off.

(8) Mr. Mike Jackson made them call me back from lay off.

(9) Mr. Lee Wilson allowed Mr. Lynn Harner to involuntary terminate me for something that other supervisors and employees did without my permission.

(10) This caused me to lose health insurance on my family.

(11) It caused hardship upon my family and me.

(12) They said I had poor performance in workmenship. These documents show a different thing from what has been told. This production pay is from when I was supervising the P-175 glass house, which was paid every two weeks, without any help to get production started from any of my superiors. They denied almost everything that I needed to perform.

	Dept	Win Units week1	$ Bonus week 1	Win Units week2	$ Bonus week 2	Actual UPMH week 1	Actual UPMH week 2	UPMH Goal	Actual Scrap % week 1	Actual Scrap % week 2	Scrap % Goal	$ UPMH Bonus	$ Scrap Bonus	Total Bonus
Brown, George	GH 3	17345	179.46	14545	148.48	9.66	8.65	8	6.41	4.15	5	81.985	37.12	$447.05

This is my production pay from June 2000, before Mr. Reed started his attacks to try to demote me for anything. They couldn't find anything, but I was demoted anyway. It hurt the company due to reduction in production, mishaps, and a lack of knowledge.

george

MONTHLY INCENTIVE PAY--MILLEN

MONTH: Mar-00

NAME : George Brown
DEPARTMENT : Glass #4 255/165

	BONUS RATE	WEEK 1	WEEK 2	WEEK 3	WEEK 4	WEEK 5	TOTAL MONTH	GOAL	BONUS
UNITS/MAN HOUR	$150	15.24	14.46	16.09	15.52	13.43	14.95	14.00	$150.00
Glass SCRAP	$150	11.1	12	12.2	11.7	13	12.0%	12.5%	$150.00
COST per Glass Pnl	$120	0.99	1	0.92	0.98	0.91	$0.96	$1.00	$120.00
SHIP COMPLETE	$100	99.5%	100.0%	99.5%	99.4%	98.8%	99.4%	98.5%	$100.00
HOUSEKEEPING	$100	28	29	28	29	29	143	104/105	$100.00
OSHA REPORTABLE	$100	0	0	0	0		0	0	$100.00
TOTAL	$720								$720.00

4 week month --- 105 to 120 pts. = full bonus   5 week month -- 132 to 150 pts. = full bonus
                  89 to 104 pts. = 1/2 bonus   113 to 131 pts. = 1/2 bonus

Page 10

This form here doesn't tell me that I had poor performance. This form tells me that this person did his job well, according to this chart. Ms. Janice Smith had these documents to go by, and she received a statement from Mr. Lee Wilson that was full of lies. The only document he had was a form that I signed, and it had been tampered with after I signed it. She could see where there were scratches through the wording on the form, and she disregarded it. She showed a lack of concern for the person's interests that filed the charge against MI.

≡PT. GLASS # 4 GEORGE BROWN		glass 4			WEEK ENDING	06|03|00			
	WDW SERIES	LABOR COST	NON-PROD. COST	FOREMAN COST	MATERIAL HANDLERS	BONUS COST	TOTAL COST	UNITS PRODUCED	COST PER UNIT
MONDAY	255	Holiday							
	165			80.00	15.00	72.08	1873.15	1802	1.04
								864	
	255	1706.07	344.25					938	
TUESDAY	255								
	165			80.00	15.00	68.24	1624.31	1706	.95
								896	
	255	1461.07	344.50					810	
WEDNESDAY	255								
	165			80.00	15.00	70.16	1820.35	1754	1.04
								530	
	255	1655.19	427.75					1324	
THURSDAY	255								
	165			80.00	15.00	81.24	1929.41	2031	.95
								1299	
	255	1753.17	543.50					732	
FRIDAY	165			0	15.00	54.40	895.95	1360	.66
								533	
	255	826.55	291.50					827	
SATURDAY	255								
	165							8653	
WEEKLY TOTALS									

Page 1

The production manager, Mr. Peter Atkinson, signed this production chart. This is somewhat of the fashion of how I performed every day unless it was caused by something beyond my control, such as tempered glass that the scheduling department didn't order on time, PP&G or the other vendors had problems and had to back order the glass, or the scheduling department ordered the wrong size glass. This management seminar certificate is not given to someone with poor performance. Would a company pay all expenses for someone to fly to Harrisburg, Pennsylvania, and book a hotel and car rental to travel back and forth from Millersburg at MI Printing Company? They wouldn't pay for meals, and entertainment, not once but twice. Ms. Smith had all of this as proof of my performance, and I still couldn't get my job back. How can one say that I had poor performance when I have received two certificates for performance, which were signed by Mr. Pete Desoto himself? I always wonder where Mr. Wilson and Ms. Smith got their information from. Was it something that they just made up? You look at the facts for yourself and come to your own conclusion.

presented to

George Brown

*in recognition for having successfully completed
the Excellent Manager Level 2 - Training Program
Presented by Performance Industries*

_____
Program Coordinator

_____
President, MI Home Products, Inc.

_____
November 1, 2 & 3, 1999
Date

Mr. Mike Jackson was the reason I was called back to work in June 2003. I wrote him and told him that they replaced me with an employee who didn't know anything about cutting. He questioned Mr. Wilson about it. They moved him and put Alphonzo Sapp there. He too had less experience than I had. He had more company violations against him than I did, such as tardiness, absentees, and misconduct regarding rules and regulations. The only write-up I had was one they brought back from the past. Mr. Todd Reed and Mr. Lee Wilson were doing everything within their power to keep me from coming back to MI Home Product Inc. Mr. Mike Jackson was the person who actually recalled me back to work.

MI Home Products, Inc.
650 West Market Street
P.O. Box 370
Gratz, PA 17030-0370

717. 365 3300
717. 365 3596 Fax

Mike Jackson
President

March 31, 2003

Mr. George Brown
P.O. Box 576
Twin City, GA 30471

Dear George,

Thank you for your letter of March 21, 2003. I appreciate your years of service and the different roles that you served. Please understand that your layoff was the direct result of organizational restructuring and the elimination of the position that you filled through consolidation.

Also, please be aware that your name is on the list of employees to be called back to work once the Millen volume levels justify the call back. Please feel free to keep in contact with Lee Wilson at the Millen plant relative to your status.

Sincerely,

Mike Jackson

MJ:csa

cc: Lee Wilson – Millen
        Todd Reed – Millen